LIFE ON MARSH

LIFE ON MARSH

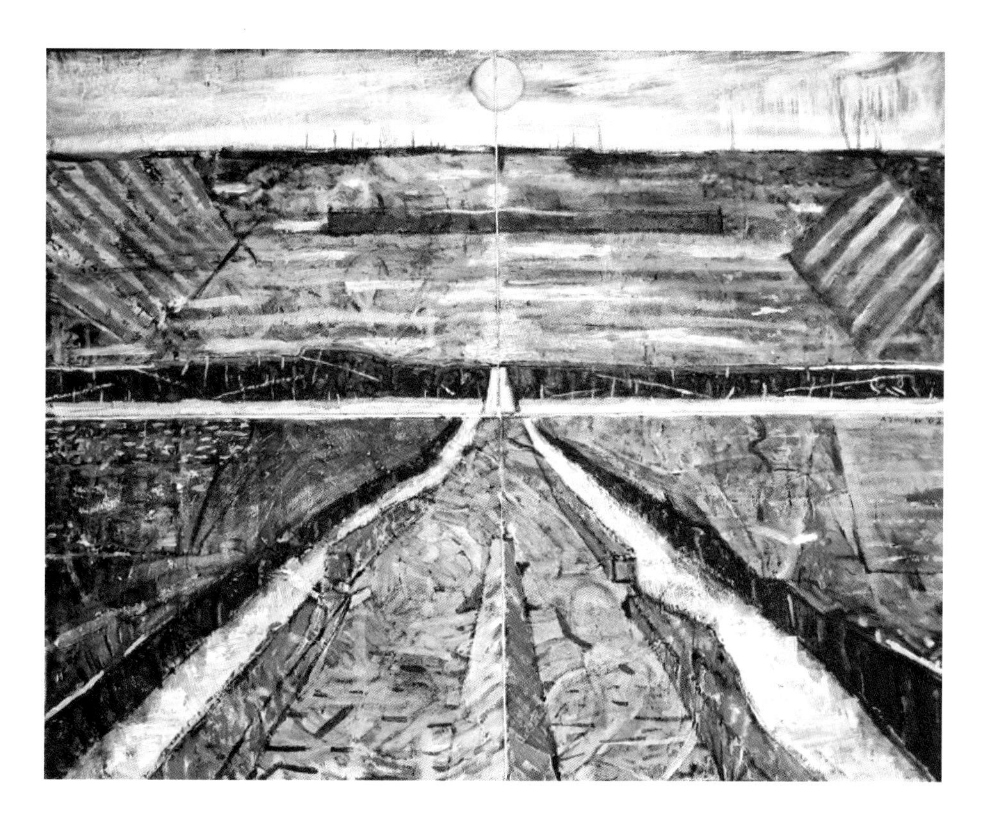

NIKO MIAOULIS &
ANDY HOLYER

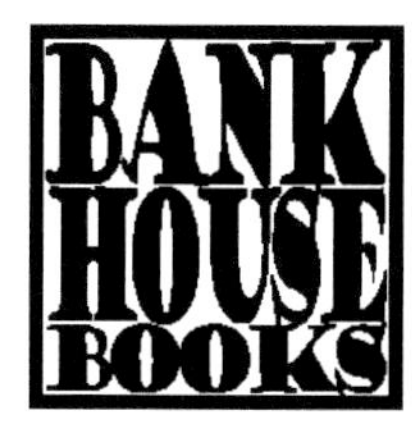

LIFE ON MARSH

First published by BANK HOUSE BOOKS 2008

ISBN 9781904408383

Production design: Dave Randle
Sir Donald Sinden portrait by June Mendoza www.junemendoza.co.uk

Designed and typeset in England by

BANK HOUSE BOOKS
BIC House
1 Christopher Road
East Grinstead
West Sussex RH19 3BT

BANK HOUSE BOOKS is a division of BANK HOUSE MEDIA LIMITED

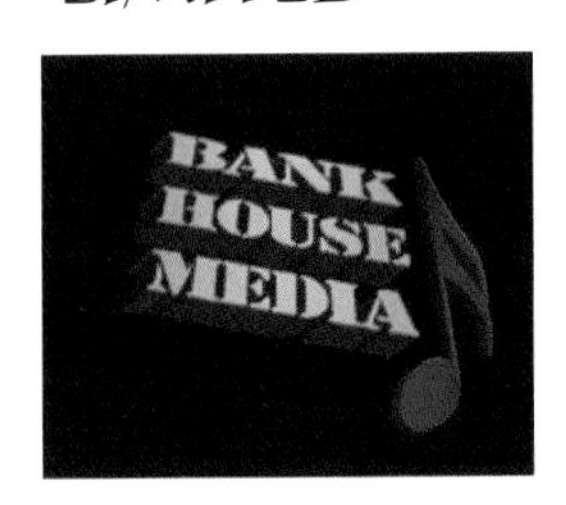

CONTENTS

To **Jenny**

'If not for you…'
with love
Andy

To **Rachel**

with all my love
and more
Niko

FOREWORD BY SIR DONALD SINDEN

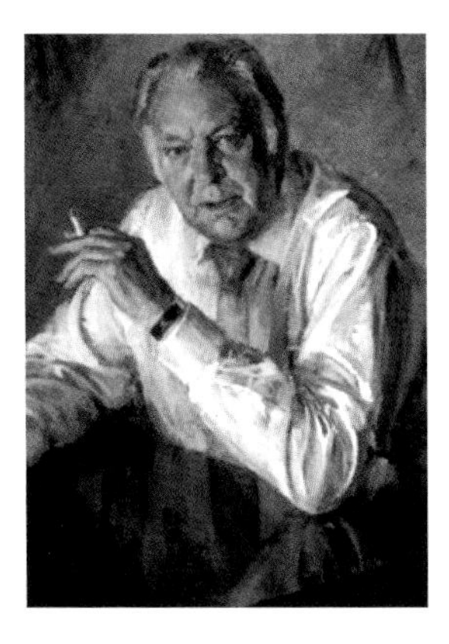

I had been a neighbour in Chelsea of actor and author Russell Thorndike, who told me of the magic of Dymchurch and the Marsh so, at his instigation, in 1954, I bought the house in which I still live.

Later, in 1960, Russell played the pirate Smee to my Captain Hook in Peter Pan at the Scala Theatre in London. It was then that he presented duly inscribed copies of his Dr Syn books to my son Marc, but it was back in 1954 that I visited Dungeness for the first time and immediately fell under its spell – and I use the word 'spell' advisedly – perhaps 'mesmerism' could be even better. Of course this was before the power station defined its limits and ruined the scale.

Thank goodness The Pilot is still there, with Niko at the helm, its signpost showing the direction to 'the other Land's End' and, blessing upon blessing, no terrible muzak!

Niko Miaoulis and Andy Holyer, sharing their combined knowledge, have produced an enchanting book on this fascinating promontory.

My thanks and best wishes to them both.

Donald Sinden

Sir Donald Sinden, CBE

FOREWORD BY MICHAEL HOWARD

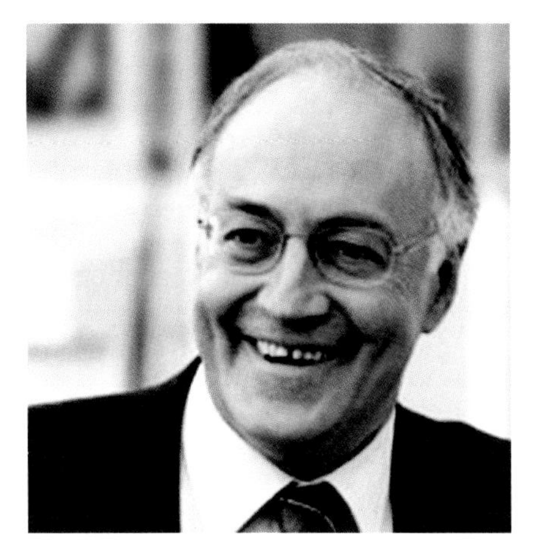

The Rt Hon Michael Howard QC MP

Romney Marsh is a hauntingly beautiful region of Britain, which it has been my privilege to serve as member of parliament for over twenty years.

For several hundred years, this land of the Cinque Ports enjoyed a degree of political and economic autonomy.

This peculiar history, combined with the Marsh's distinctive geography, has given the people of the Marsh a strong sense of identity and of place.

It is this singular synthesis of history and the environment that inspires both myself and all those who know the Marsh. I overlook it from my home and it gives me endless pleasure.

I am delighted to endorse a book which celebrates the character of the Marsh in vibrant colour and insightful prose.

Michael Howard QC MP

INTRODUCING THE FIFTH QUARTER

The Ingoldsby Legends, written by the Rev. Richard Barham in 1793, described Romney Marsh as the Fifth or Hidden Quarter. The Marsh and specifically Dungeness have a reputation for secrecy, mystery and independence that goes back thousands of years. For many of those years most sensible and honest folks stayed well away, through fear of robbery, death or malaria, known locally as the 'marsh ague'.

More recently the area has become a magnet for those seeking something very different from the hustle and bustle of today's stressful life. The area has inspired writers, artists and film makers, many of whom have made the Marsh their home.

This book combines the personal insight of Niko Miaoulis with the unique paintings of Andy Holyer, an artist born and bred on the Marsh. Both are keen amateur historians, with a passion for this unique area and its rich heritage.

They don't intend this book to be an academic work of reference. They do, however, hope that the reader will seek out further literature about the Marsh or, better still, spend some time exploring this very special place.

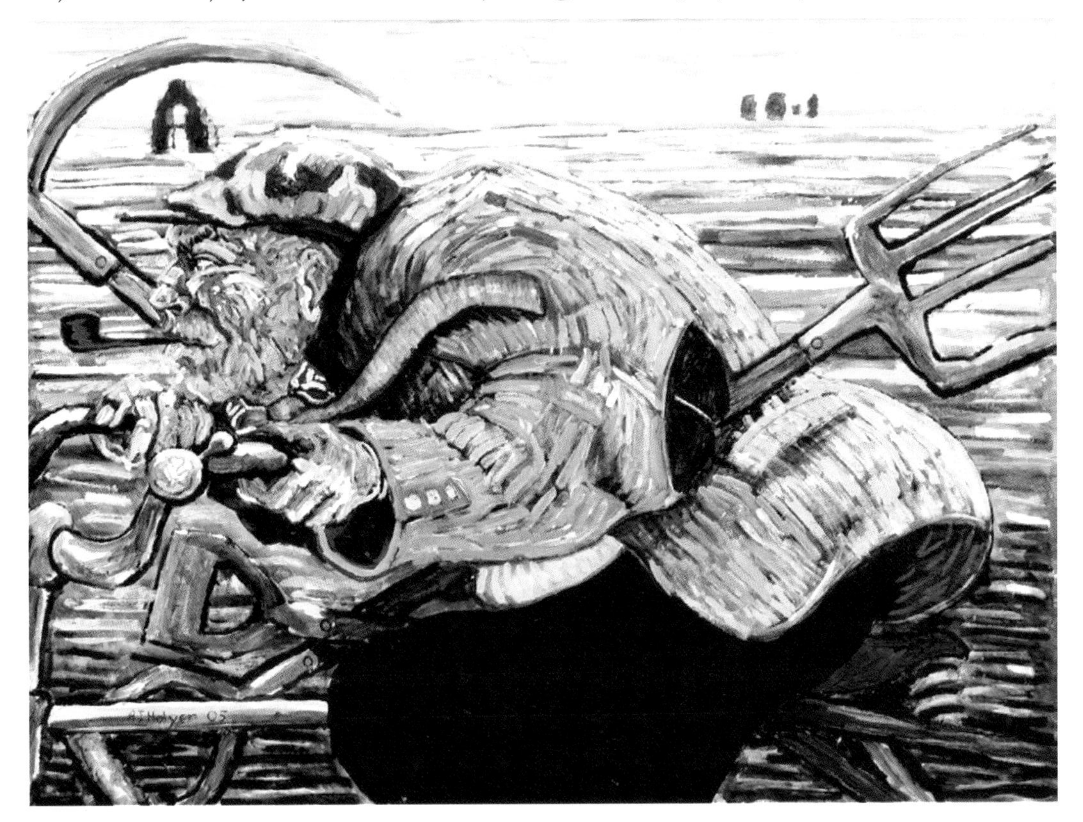

ANDY HOLYER: RETURN OF THE NATIVE

Since returning to Romney Marsh I have lived in three locations. The first was a flat overlooking Littlestone beach in a crumbling and damp relic of Edwardian splendour belonging to an era when Littlestone was to be a new Eastbourne complete with pier and pleasure gardens. Overstretched and under financed, this grandiose scheme faltered and halted. The leaking roof and peeling wallpaper of my decomposing (but cheap) accommodation were compensated for by the view to sea and the proximity of the shore.

On sun-soaked days when the tide was out (the tide goes out a long way at Littlestone in its unpatriotic attempt to reunite England with France) white weathered groynes clutched at the shingle before giving way to the sands that shimmer and sparkle mauve, ochre and turquoise under the horizon airbrushed by haze. To my left there was a mulberry harbour stranded on a sandbank unable to join its siblings on the Normandy beaches for D-Day. To my right the coast stretched around to Dungeness Point where power stations A and B stood sentry. Below me were a row of bright painted beach huts interspersed with fishing boats and old rusting winding gear.

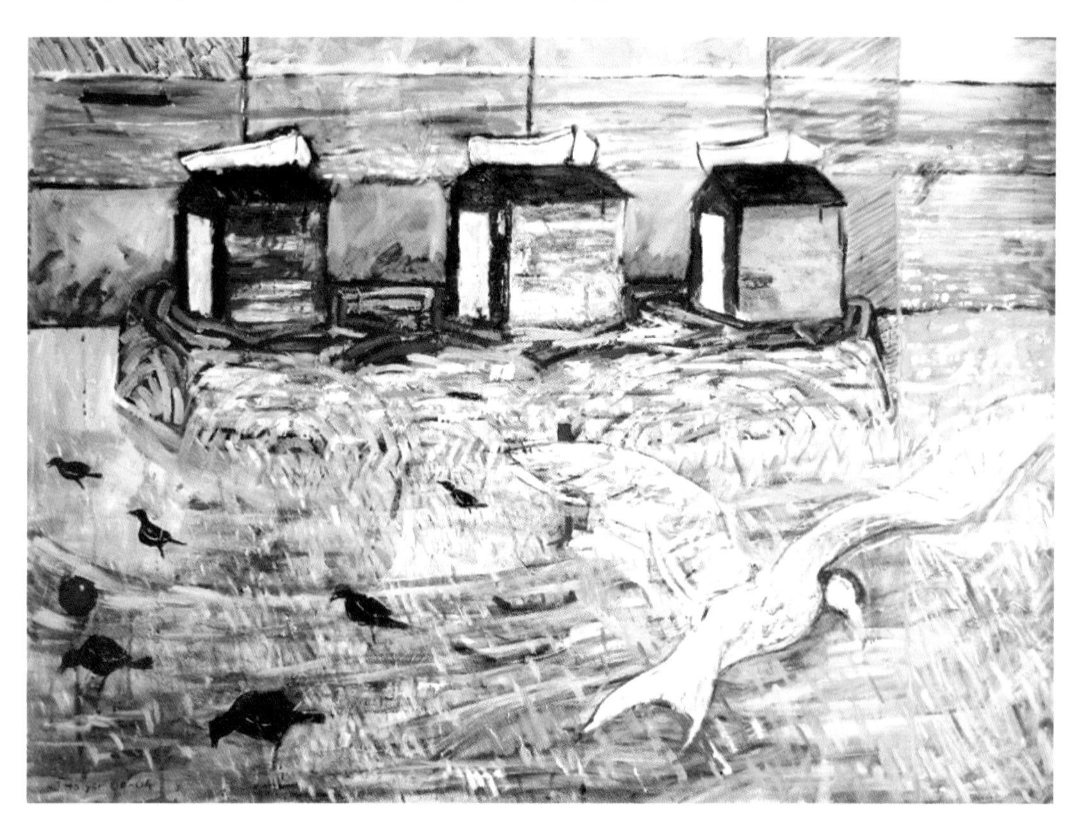

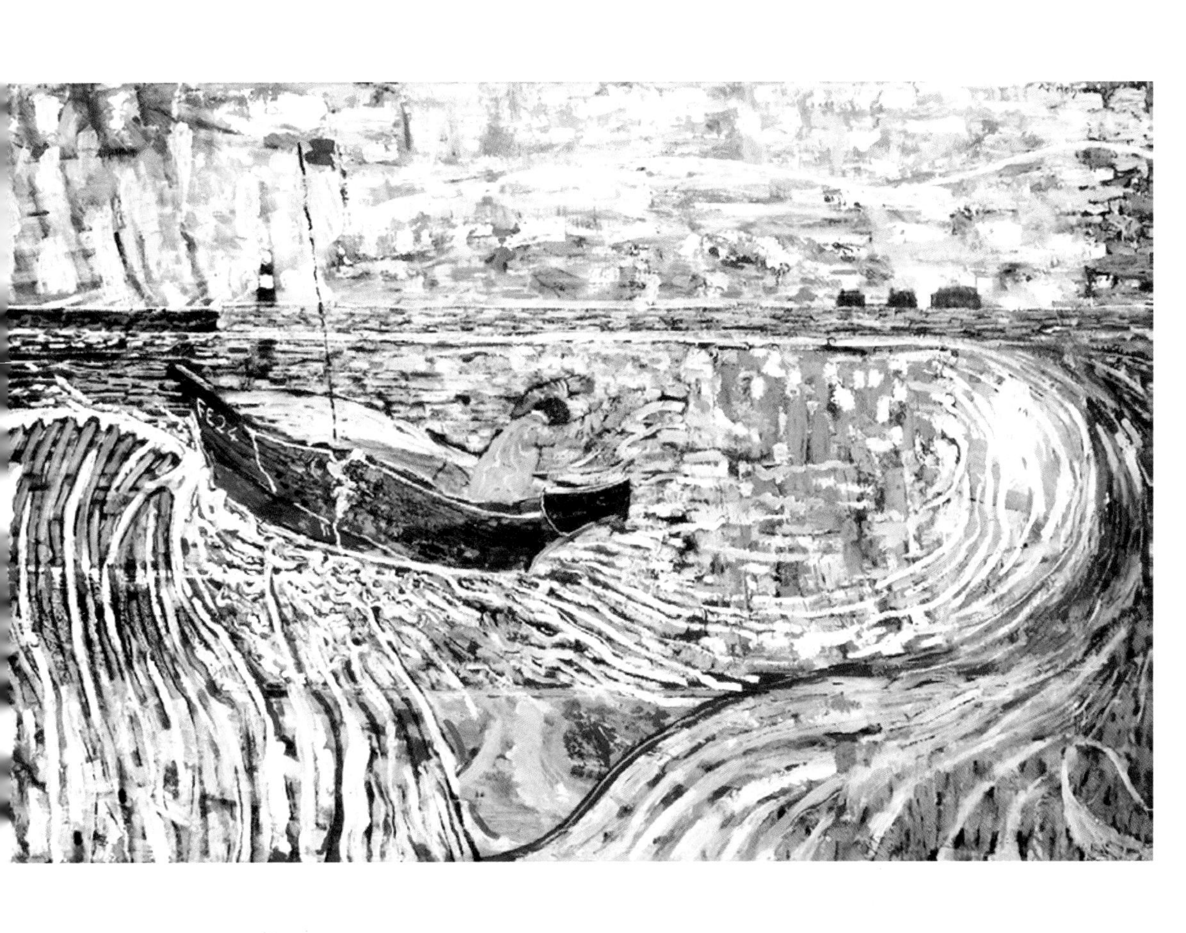
FE24

On a stormy night the atmosphere was positively Shakespearean, with the sound of shingle being crushed on the shore and the elements pounding on the window. Unfortunately fierce nature bullied its way into the flat and demanded to be put up for the night. Despite protests from local bucket vendors I felt that I needed a property with a working roof and windows that fitted into the holes.

And so to the lighthouse keeper's cottage in Dungeness. On the day of moving in it was typical Dungeness weather: 80 mph winds (with sleet). These winds sculpt the vegetation, foxes, weasels and rabbits and the human inhabitants into a cowering north-easterly position, forced into the shallow shelter of the numerous ridges of the ness. But the cottage was dry and cosy with the scent of burning driftwood on the fire and a sense of rugged isolation and peace.

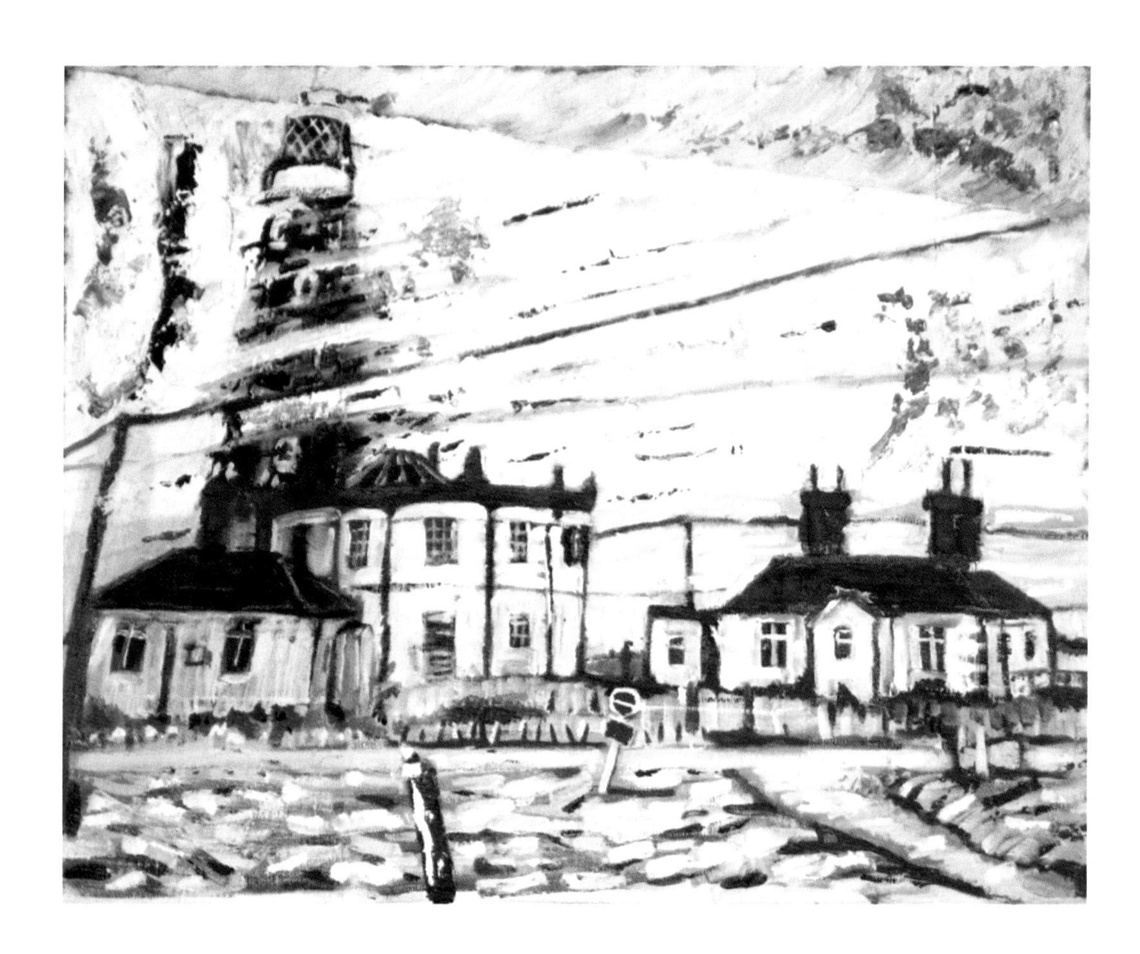

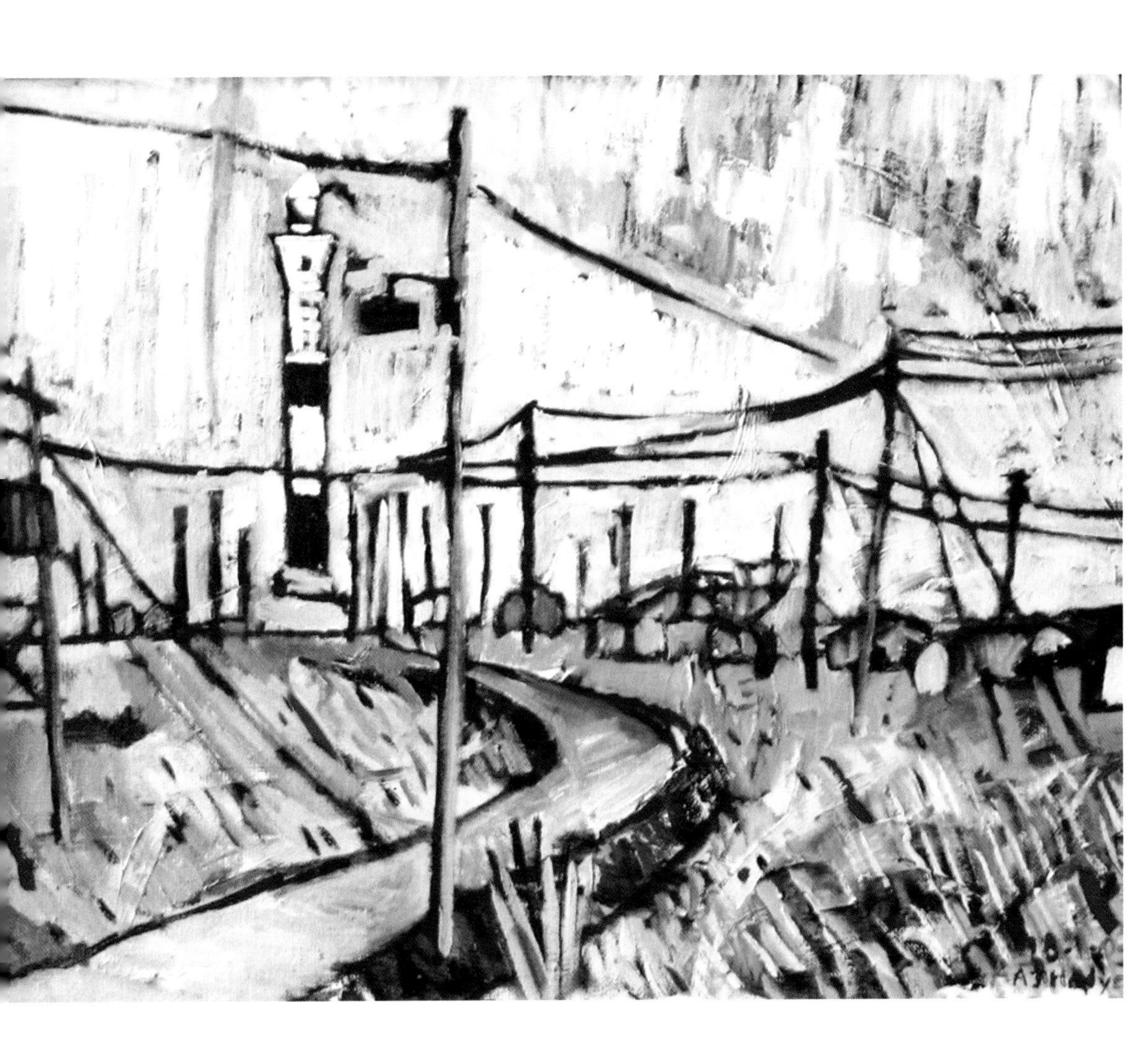

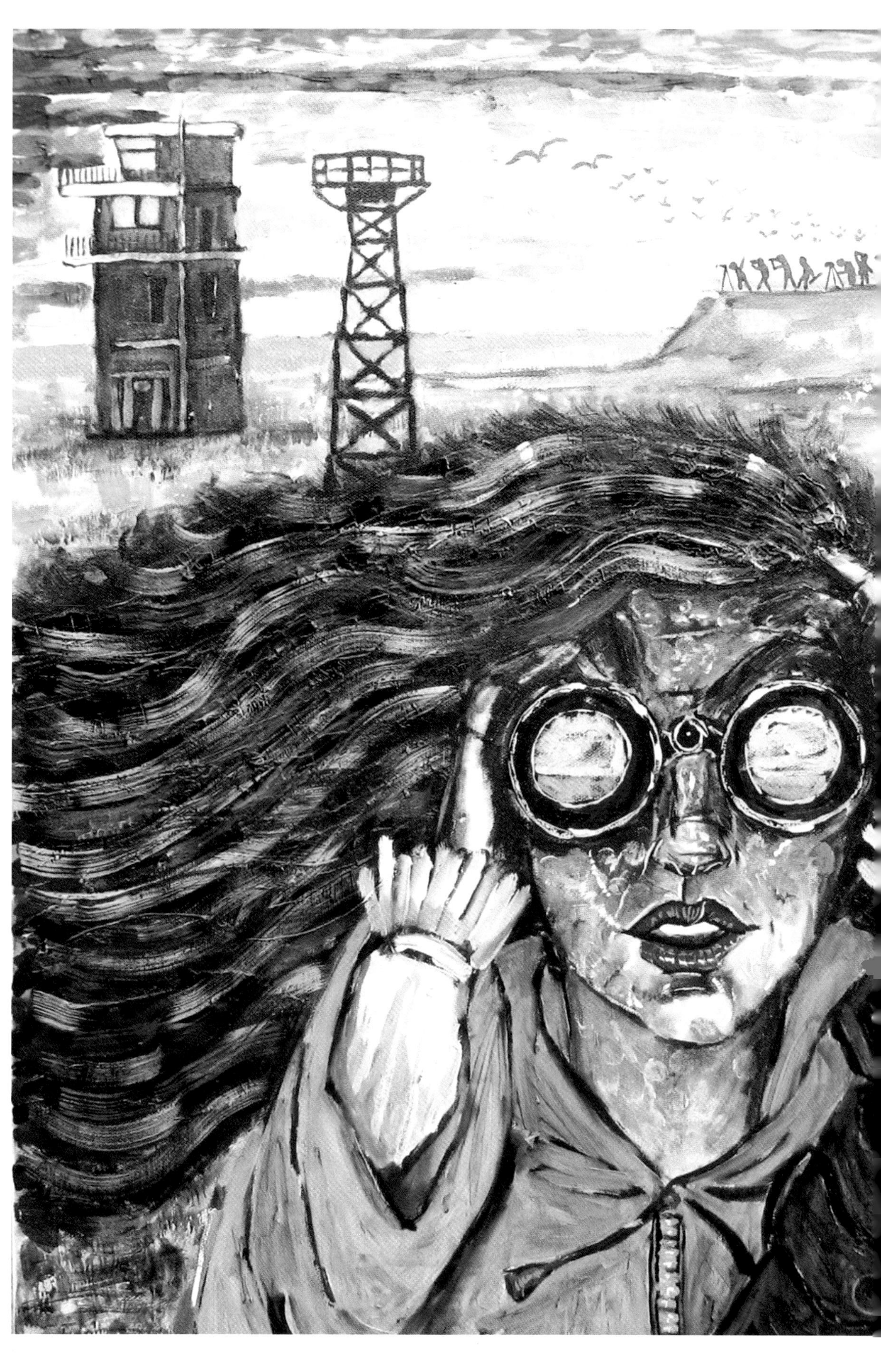

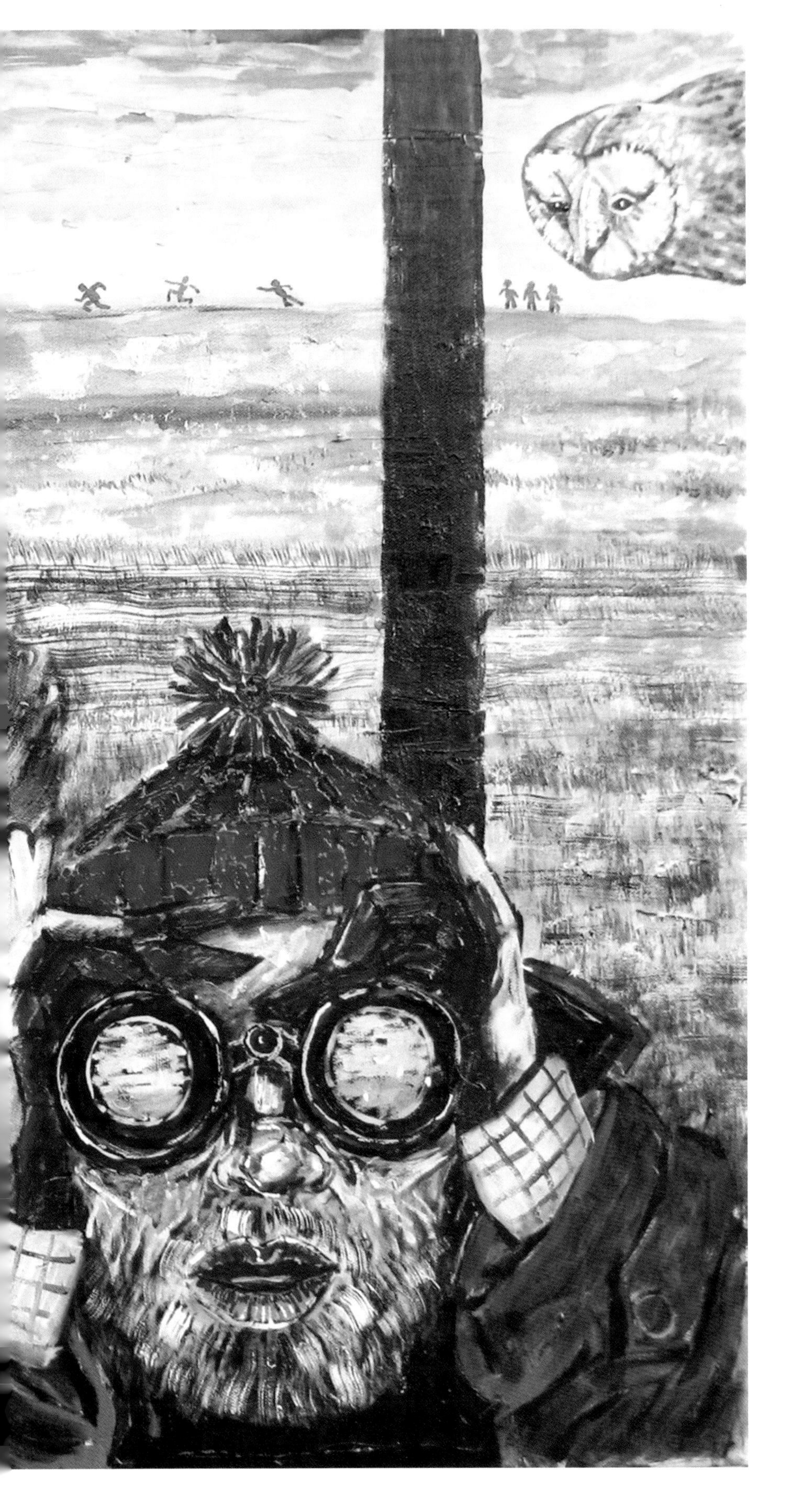

Spring at Dungeness is met with the defiant flowering of purple vipers bugloss, pink and white valerian, yellow-horned poppies and many other tenacious plants that conspire to make Dungeness sing with colour out of the unyielding stone.

Jenny and I spent three happy years there, our idyll only intruded upon, on occasion, by galloping armies of birdwatchers keen to observe a rare bird with a Latin name (to you and me a seagull, finch or duck) or the summer migration of cultural tourists, who, inspired by Derek Jarman or the lifestyle columns of the *Guardian,* make a pilgrimage to Dungeness and take endless photographs or make sketches of Jarman's cottage, the lighthouse and the decaying remains of the fishing industry. In the height of summer it felt as if we were being stalked by the paparazzi as photographers and artists concentrated their sights upon our home and garden.

Otherwise time was punctuated by the welcome but ghostly shrills and hisses of the steam engines of the Romney Hythe and Dymchurch Light Railway across the road.

Our existence was dominated by the presence of the nuclear power station, which at night seemed to be a replica of the Emerald City in the Land of Oz.

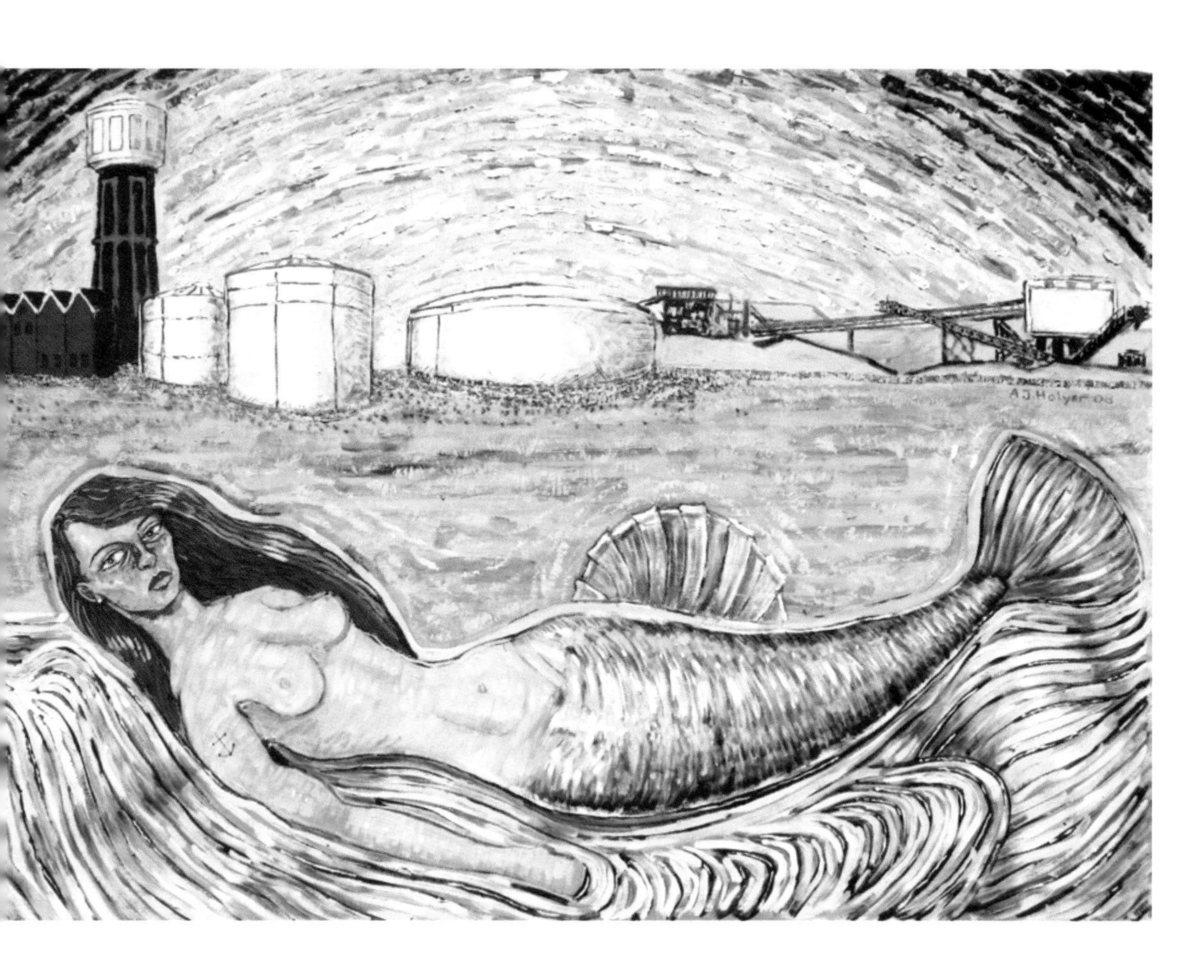
A.J.Holyer 08

Once, 'nuclear nurses' visited to hand out iodine tablets and to instruct us about what to do in the case of a nuclear accident. Apparently we were to close our doors and windows and wait for a policeman to call. We were touched by the nurse's faith in the local constabulary and indeed our perceived nonchalant attitude to radiation poisoning.

I now have a house and studio in Lydd, the nearest town to Dungeness. Whilst technically a town Lydd retains all the atmosphere of a village where everybody knows everybody or is at least related to them. There is a local joke that no one leaves the Marsh, and those that attempt to do so get a nosebleed when they reach nearby Appledore.

From Roman times until the early medieval period Lydd was an island and important fishing community and Cinque Port. A combination of land reclamation, storms that altered the course of waterways and the unstoppable drift of shingle from the west has left Lydd several miles inland.

The fishermen and shepherds (locally known as lookers) have largely gone but Lydd remains a friendly, peaceful village that maintains a quality and pace of life out of step with the 24/7 corporate world beyond its ditches, dykes and winding lanes.

Before my return to the Marsh my art had been inspired by the urban and industrial north where I used to live. I took as reference expressionist painters like Otto Dix and Max Beckman, and also the British kitchen sink realists, including John Bratby, to whom I was studio assistant.

Inevitably I came to respond to the local environment. The colours especially seep unbeckoned into the imaginative landscape. Cerulean blue, purple, gold and white are mirrored in the wide sea and tall sky. Set amongst this abstract expressionist canvas man's mark is stark and often surreal. Skeletal churches, lighthouses, electrical pylons and the rusted remains of agricultural and fishing industries struggle to order and frame an otherwise infinitely open and formless vista.

Consequently I now find that I relate more strongly to the neo-romantic and surreal tradition of British Art.

Alongside the visceral thrill of the geography came the increased obsession

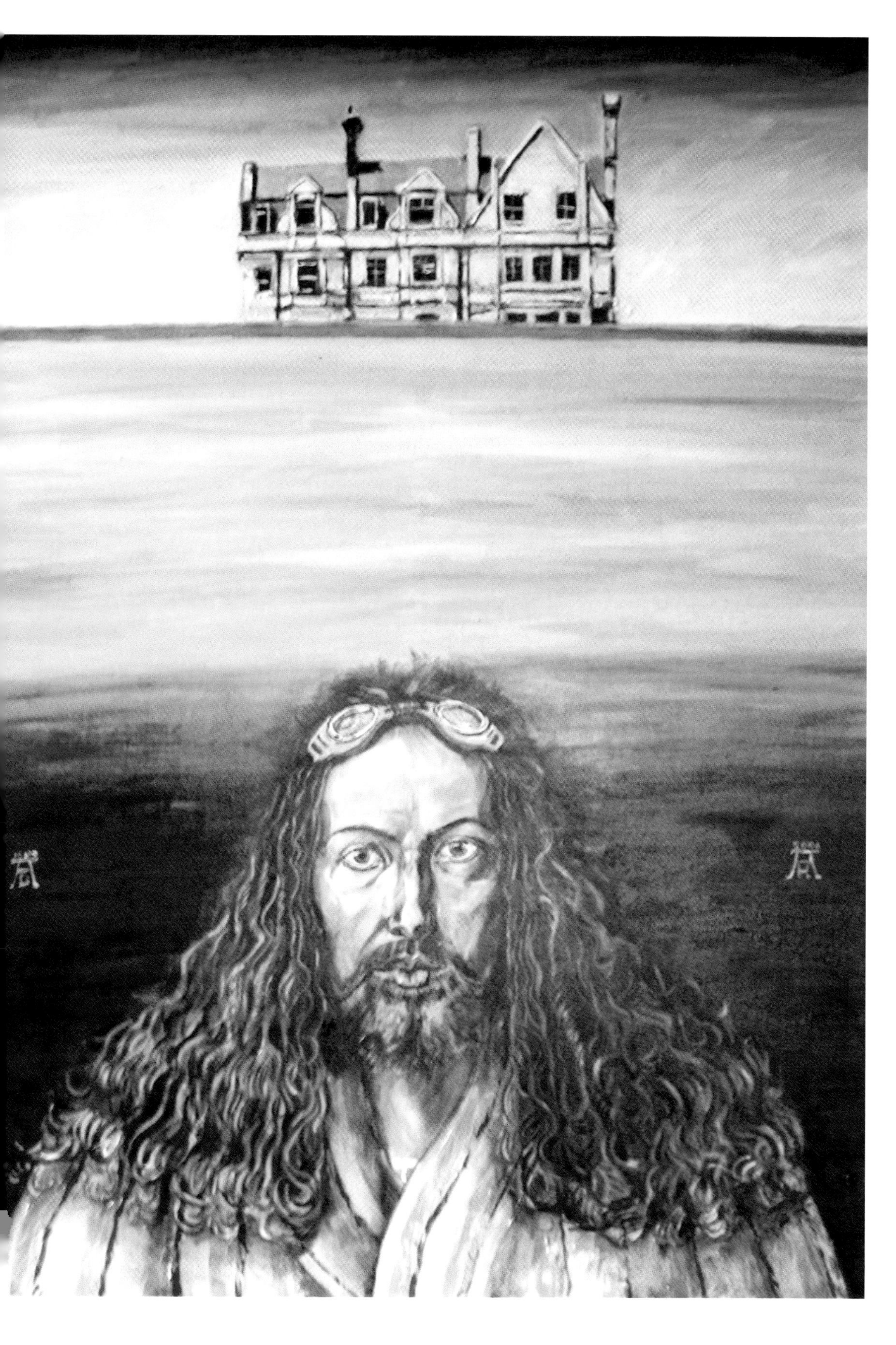

with the history of the Marsh and its people. Perhaps it is something to do with being the returning native that makes one so fascinated with a cultural inheritance that those who live cheek by jowl with it take for granted and don't feel compelled to comment upon.

It is perhaps because of the Marsh's isolation from centres of learning that its social history is not widely recorded or celebrated. In recent years historians like Ann Roper, Jill Eddison, John Carpenter and Margaret Bird have tried to make a record of ancient history and 'living' history, but much remains tantalising conjecture. History has often been recorded by writers who are relying on folklore or their own interpretations of unacknowledged sources.

Niko Miaoulis and I first started sharing our enthusiasm for finding out more about this place, this last of England, over a pint in the Pilot Inn. We swapped books, artefacts and anecdotes about the area and speculated upon what was and what might have been, aided and abetted by a rich vein of local knowledge that passed by the bar.

It therefore seemed fitting to set down in a book at least some of the things that we find inspirational about Romney Marsh and Dungeness.

So if the reader is sitting comfortably, I will hand you over to mine host Niko who will tell you tales of the Fifth Quarter, most of which are true.

Andy Holyer, August 2008

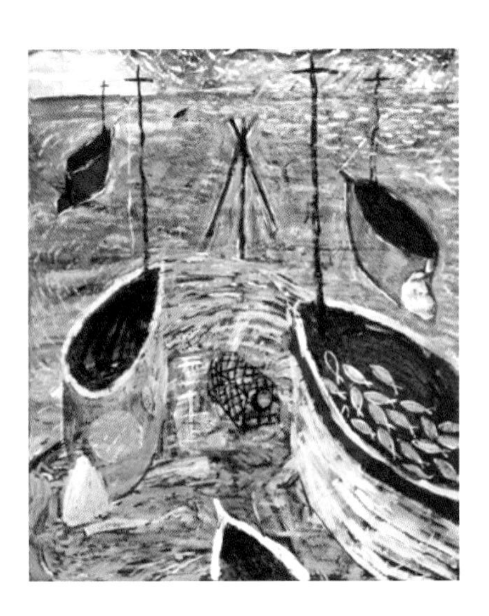

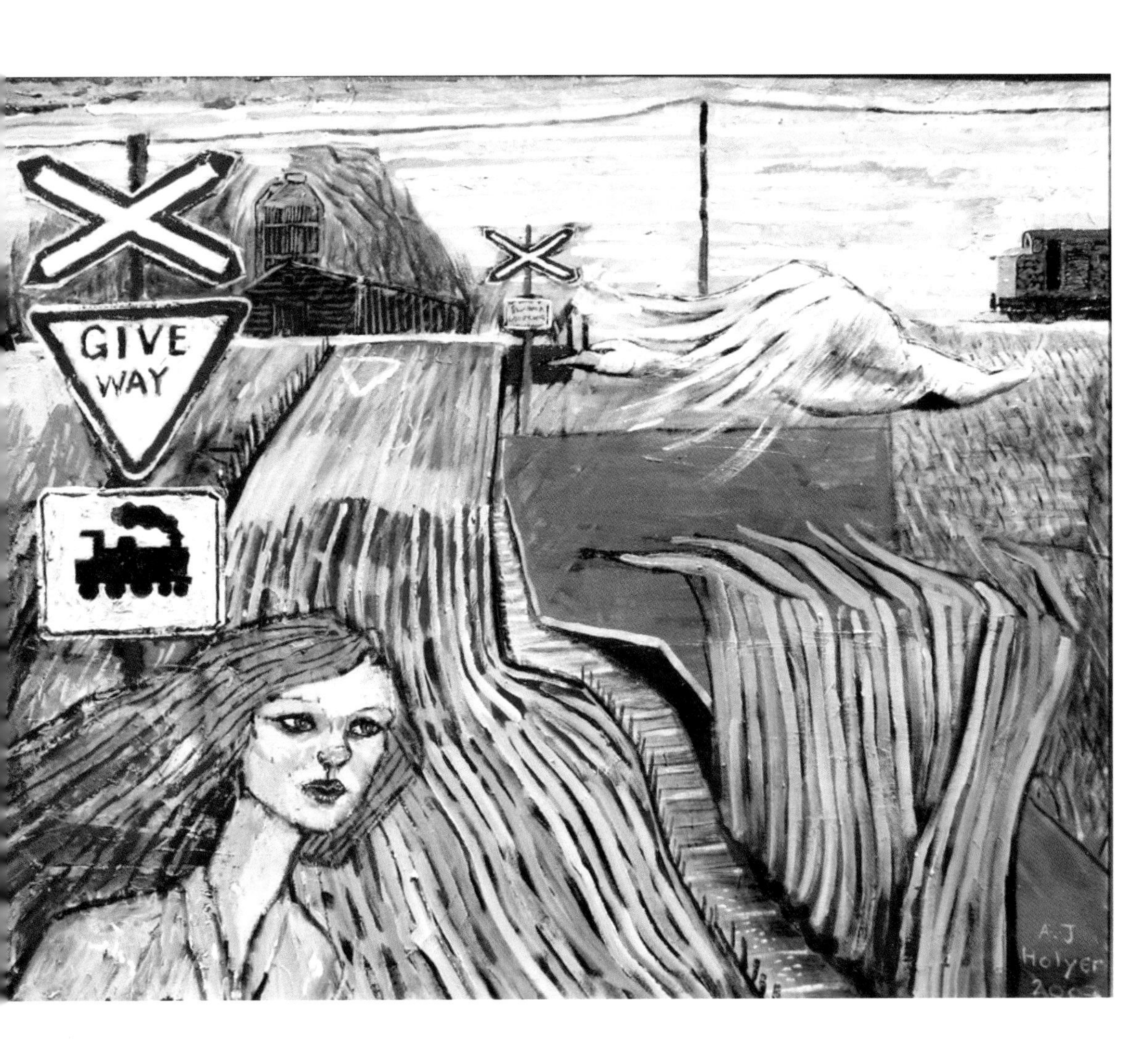
GIVE
WAY
A.J
Holyer

OF FIRESHIPS AND FISH AND CHIPS

NIKO MIAOULIS

Not being particularly superstitious, it is a source of great mystery to me how it seemed to be inevitable that my life would become inextricably linked with Dungeness – like the flint pebbles which are wrenched out of the chalk cliffs hundreds of miles away in Dorset, to begin their inch by inch sightseeing tour of England's whole south coast, rolling up and down every inch of beach, drifting ever eastwards until they are reunited with their brethren at Dungeness, where at last they will have found rest and purpose.

In much the same way I have spent my forty-three years drifting southwards as if pulled by a magnet, until my journey ended in Dungeness. Here I have found the brethren that I have always craved and the purpose that has unconsciously driven me here, along with a heritage that is closely linked with my ancestry and enough history and mystery to keep me going until the end of my days.

In many ways my life until Dungeness seemed to be educating me and preparing me for the day when I would finally succumb to the inevitable. When it actually happened it really was like a jolt or bolt of realisation that this was what it was all about.

My life started somewhat inauspiciously as the first born son of Greek immigrant parents. Blissfully unaware of my geographical destiny, I was brought up in Scotland, in and around Edinburgh. In the 1970s Scotland was not as cosmopolitan and accepting of difference as it is now.

The only respite seemed to be the yearly family holiday to Greece where I felt much more accepted and at home (even with my Scottish accent!). It was on these yearly trips that I learned to appreciate my family heritage and the esteem that we were held in by the Greek nation. My great, great, great grandfather was the legendary Admiral Andreas Miaoulis. Born in 1768 and capitalising on his family's seafaring heritage, he quickly built up a formidable trading fleet and became an extremely rich man. By taking risks in running cargo to and from war zones and blockaded areas, he developed a reputation for great feats of seamanship under the most difficult of conditions. He was extremely well travelled by the standards of the day, and lived in France for a

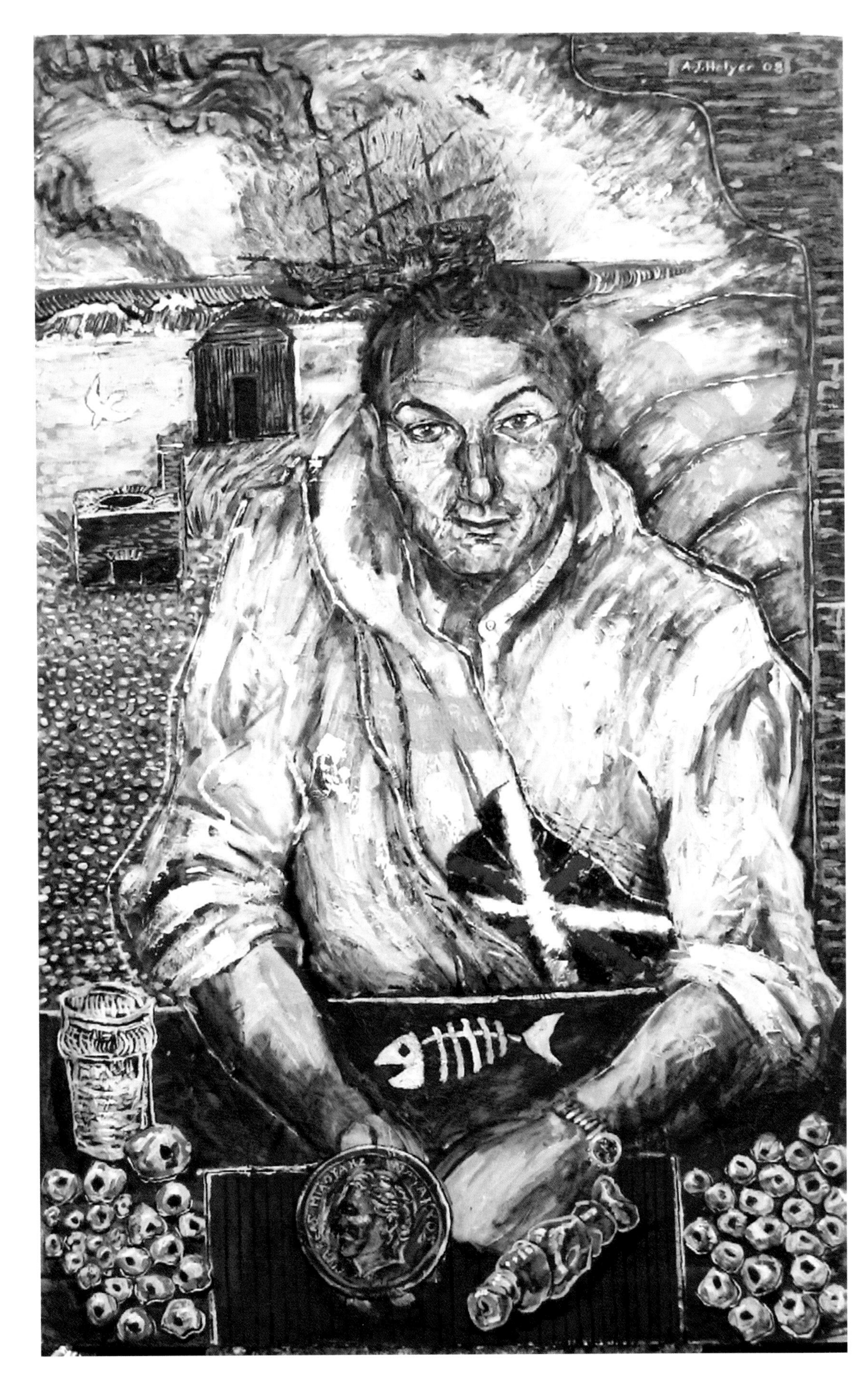
A.J.Helyer 08

number of years; he spoke several languages. Miaoulis was also a personal friend of Admiral Nelson.

In 1821 when he was nearly fifty his life was to change dramatically. The Ottoman Turks had occupied Greece for over 300 years; their rule was oppressive and often murderous, clearing whole islands of their populations, executing the men and shipping the women and children to the markets of the east to be sold off as slaves and prostitutes. Miaoulis was one of the prime movers who triggered the Greeks to revolt against their cruel oppressors. He sold everything he owned to build a fleet of warships and to hire the sailors to crew them and quickly acquired a fearsome reputation for his audacious method of sinking Turkish ships.

Although the Greek ships were much smaller and had far fewer guns, Miaoulis would fill one of his ships up with gunpowder, tar and anything else that would burn. He would then set the ship alight and ram it into the larger Turkish vessel, usually under a murderous hail of fire. Having dealt a fatal blow to the ship, he would then escape in a small rowing boat. He was to sink many Turkish ships in this way. The Turks understandably became very wary of him, often preferring to turn and sail back to Turkey or Egypt on encountering Miaoulis's fleet.

Miaoulis lived to see Greece freed from the Muslims in 1827. Even in his sixties he was still at the forefront of political affairs. After the assassination of the first prime minister of Greece the country descended into civil war, torn between siding with the British or the Russians. The pride of the Greek navy was a ship called *Hellas*, which was gifted to Miaoulis by the United States. Rather than give up his beautiful new ship to the then dominant Russian faction, he scuttled it and set it on fire in Poros harbour in front of a horrified senior delegation. This act was one of the catalysts that finally brought the country to its senses, allowing it to become the modern, western country that it is today. Miaoulis was one of the five Greek statesmen who travelled to Germany to formally invite the newly appointed king to take the crown of Greece. Miaoulis's son Athanasios was to become Greek prime minister twice.

In a relatively small country with a recent and well-documented war of independence, heritage and respect are paramount. My relations in Greece have all been involved in the naval tradition, some at a senior level, and have the sea in their blood; most of them have earned their living through fishing at some time in their lives and it is a recurring theme in our family. The name Miaoulis is held in great esteem amongst Greeks. I was always somewhat bemused when on finding out my family name a Greek would warmly embrace me, launching into in-depth analysis of some obscure sea battle that took place nearly 200 years ago. Often I would be (and still often am) compelled to shake the hand of other friends or relations, or even dragged forcibly into total strangers' houses for drinks or food (Greeks are very hospitable, you know!). All this attention in Greece made my returning home to Scotland a bit of a downer, as you can imagine.

The whole negative of being perceived as different at school suddenly became a huge positive in the employment market. It enabled me to be noticed in a positive way. Suddenly, all the years of being immersed in books came to fruition. I quickly found an ability to speak and convince others, along with an affinity with all things electromechanical.

At the age of twenty four I moved to Kent with my future wife Rachel to take on the engineering manager's role in a new Microchip plant. At this time I also found I had an ability to be quite creative, and the first evidence of this at that time, was to achieve a series of patents on some very detailed semiconductor engineering solutions.

Over the years I drifted slowly southeast taking on more and more senior roles, each one being less fulfilling than the last, and each one paying more, resulting in my various employers having ever more of a hold over my time and life. One day Rachel announced she had had enough of her corporate life and that we both needed to get some perspective on what the important things in life were.

We had been to The Pilot many times. We knew some of the locals, we loved the area, we knew it was up for sale, so we bought it for Rachel, just like that!

Initially, I could not bring myself to give up my "glamorous", highly paid but extremely stressful role running a very large company's software business for Europe, but as time went on the pull of Dungeness got to me. Jonathan was born around this time and I was not really able to spend any quality time with him. I vividly remember my torturous five hour a day commute; the closer I got to Dungeness the more relaxed and at home I felt. And, arriving there, I knew

I was where I belonged. Having the sea all around felt normal and natural, and watching the ever changing weather became a source of fascination. The local residents, talked the same nautical language and had the same heritage as my ancestors. This was the place for me.

Although financially the day job was extremely attractive, the longer I spent away from Dungeness the more out of place I felt. Sitting in a room full of power dressed "somebodys" conducting meetings about which plants to close and where to build new ones costing billions of dollars, I became increasingly detached from the reality that existed in Dungeness. In the end my heart just wasn't in it, and it was surprisingly easy to throw in the towel on "the dream job" at age thirty nine. In the last few months, on the days that I managed to make it into the office (which was a 200 mile round trip on the M25), I was so laid back that I was attending meetings dressed more appropriately for a fishing trip off Dungeness. I gently eased myself out over a period of months and then one day, I just didn't go back in.

That was it, I had come home at last.

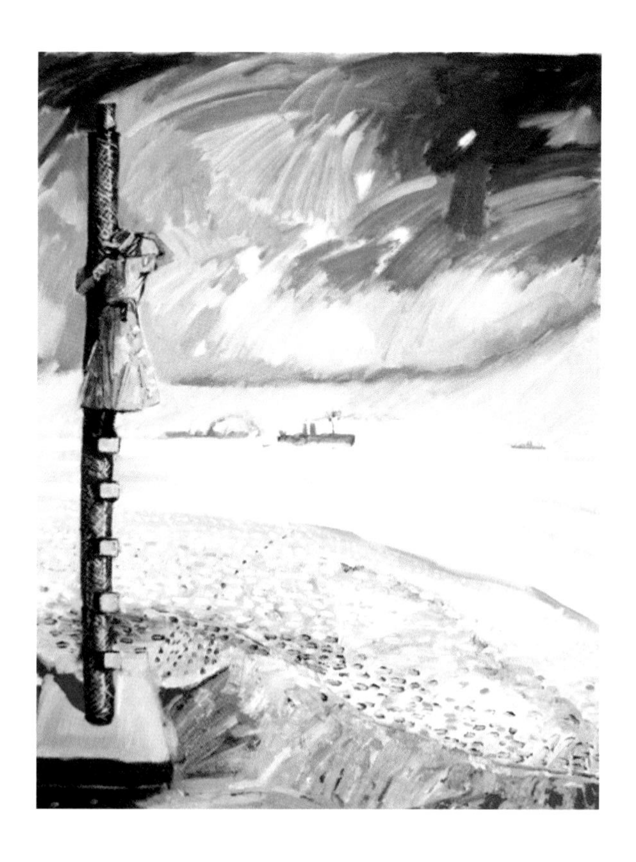

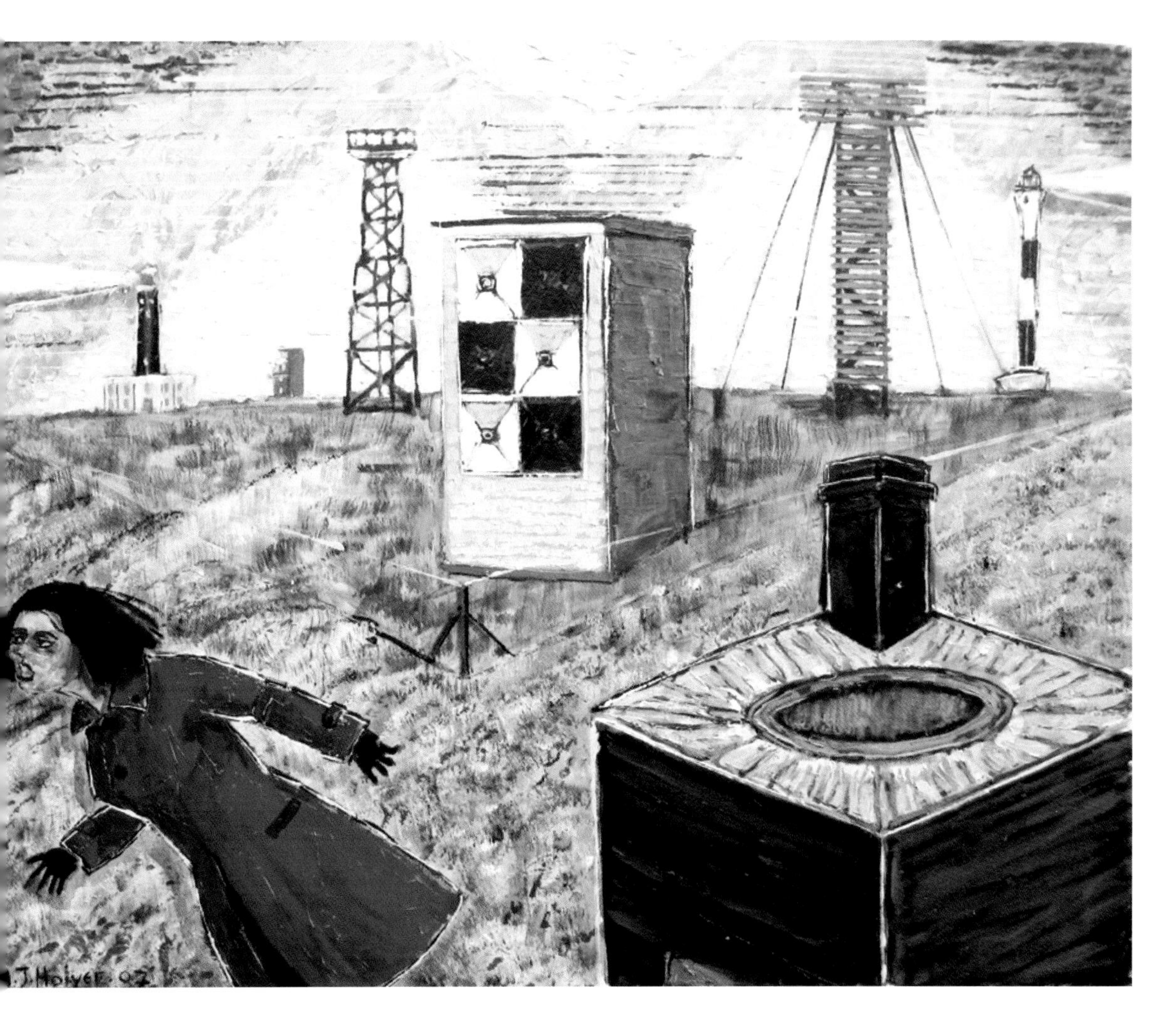

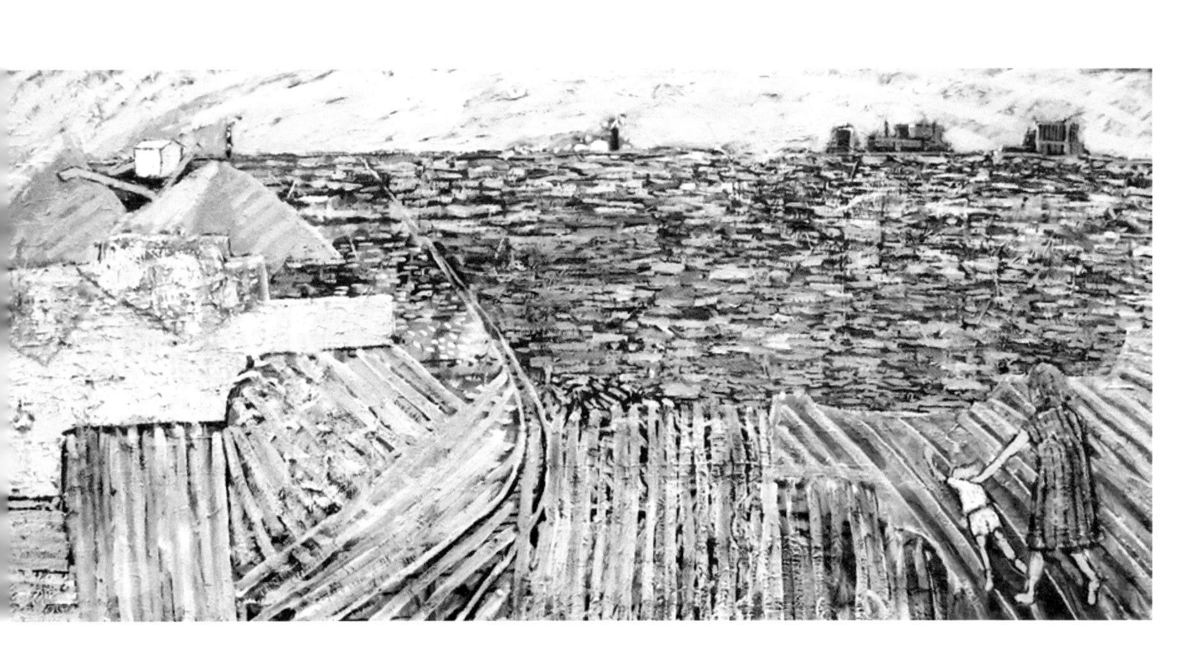

THE PILOT INN

There has been a public house on Dungeness since at least 1633; local lore says that it was then known as the Dover Hoveller. The proper definition of a hovel is a hut or upturned old boat, which a hoveller used a shelter whence he could sit and scan the sea. Most hovels were roomy and snug enough, even in rough weather, and although intended chiefly as a place of outlook, they nevertheless had sundry conveniences which made them more comfortable than the average home of the time. The owners of these nautical huts dwelt in them, hence the name 'hoveller'. Hovellers' main purpose in life was to go off to ships in distress and to wrecks, in which dangerous occupation they were successful in annually saving much property and many human lives. Their livelihood from salvage was very precarious. Sometimes they were 'flush with cash', while at other more barren times they were perhaps not as quite rigorous in declaring their salvage, or in saving lives at the expense of valuable pickings. It was also not unknown for them to supplement their income by trading illicit and contraband goods.

The original name of The Pilot ties in very nicely with its history. There is documentary evidence going back at least 150 years that the main bar building of The Pilot was constructed by upturning the hull of a Spanish ship called the *Alfresia,* which was deliberately wrecked by the locals in 1633. They murdered the crew and stole the cargo of brandy and gold. Many old photographs show that the original building was indeed made from what looks like the hull of a boat; the timber spars can be clearly seen in pictures inside The Pilot. When the New Pilot was built in 1958 the interior was constructed with curved ceilings and large beams to carry on the tradition.

The Pilot's changing name follows the history of Dungeness itself. The whole area had been involved in smuggling, wrecking and other illegal practices until it made a 180 degree turn in its outlook, and started to protect shipping rather than preying on it. In the mid- to late nineteenth century, when Channel pilots were living at and working out of the premises, their sole purpose being to give safe passage to all shipping traversing the very dangerous waters around Dungeness, the pub changed its name to The Pilot. Many of the pub's owners and residents since that time have been the backbone of the distinguished Dungeness lifeboat crew, which until recently was one of the most active of all UK lifeboats – saving thousands of lives over the years.

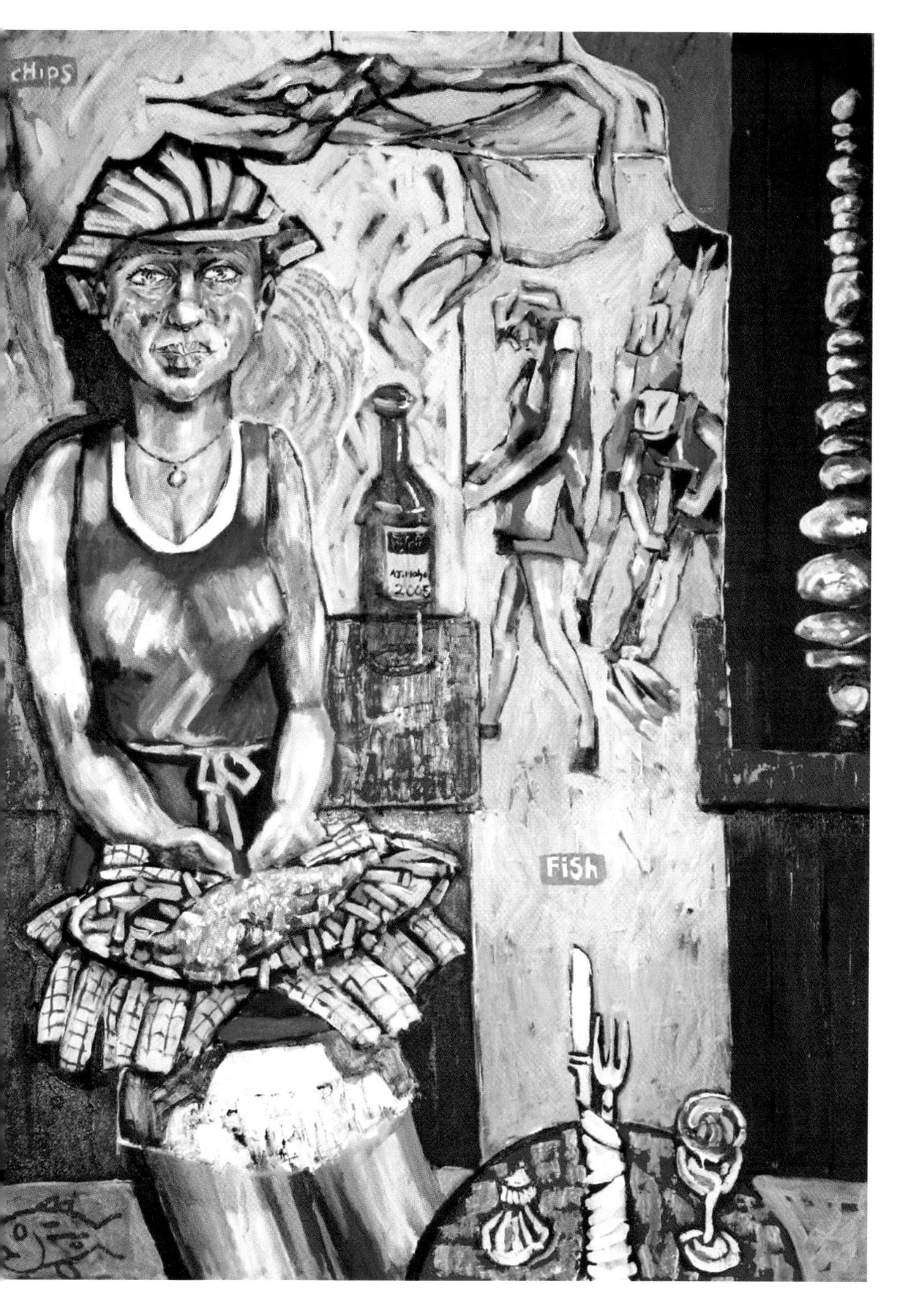
cHips
2005
FiSh

CINQUE, SUNK AND SCOT FREE

Dungeness and the surrounding area have seen massive changes in their topography in the last 1000 years. These changes contrast with most other areas in the UK which only morph slowly through millennia. The constant threat of the land being totally reshaped could be viewed as similar to living on the slopes of an active volcano.

Two thousand years ago the whole area of Romney Marsh was open sea, apart from a single long thin spit of shingle stretching from Rye to where Dungeness is now.

At the time of the Roman invasion nearly two thousand years ago the sea level was still dropping as a consequence of the last ice age. The Romans quickly recognised the potential value of this fertile land, and started a drainage programme that continues to this day. Initially the Romans built large walls to drain the areas easily defended from the sea. After the Romans left in 400AD the locals, having fewer resources and less manpower, resorted to 'inning', which involved very small-scale draining and flood protection by individual families. This practice resulted in a patchwork system of tiny fields, some of which can still be seen today.

After the Romans left much of England descended into anarchy, and Romney Marsh was no exception. In the time before the Norman Conquest in 1066 the whole of the Marsh was in the hands of the Merscwara, a fearsome warlike tribe who marked the boundary of their territory with carved lions atop stone pillars, according to the Dark Age cleric Nennius.

Even when the Norman Conquest came, most people kept well away from the area – allowing it to govern itself except for the most serious of issues. Indeed this was formalised with the establishment of the Cinque Ports, a system of local independent governance. In return for the privilege of a local judicial system and tax raising powers (the 'scots' from which the wily could get away with, hence 'scot free'), the Cinque Port towns provided ships and men for the defence of the realm.

In the twelfth and thirteenth centuries there was a series of devastating floods which shaped much of the Marsh's present day topography. The town of Romney was one of the worst affected. The river Rother used to run through

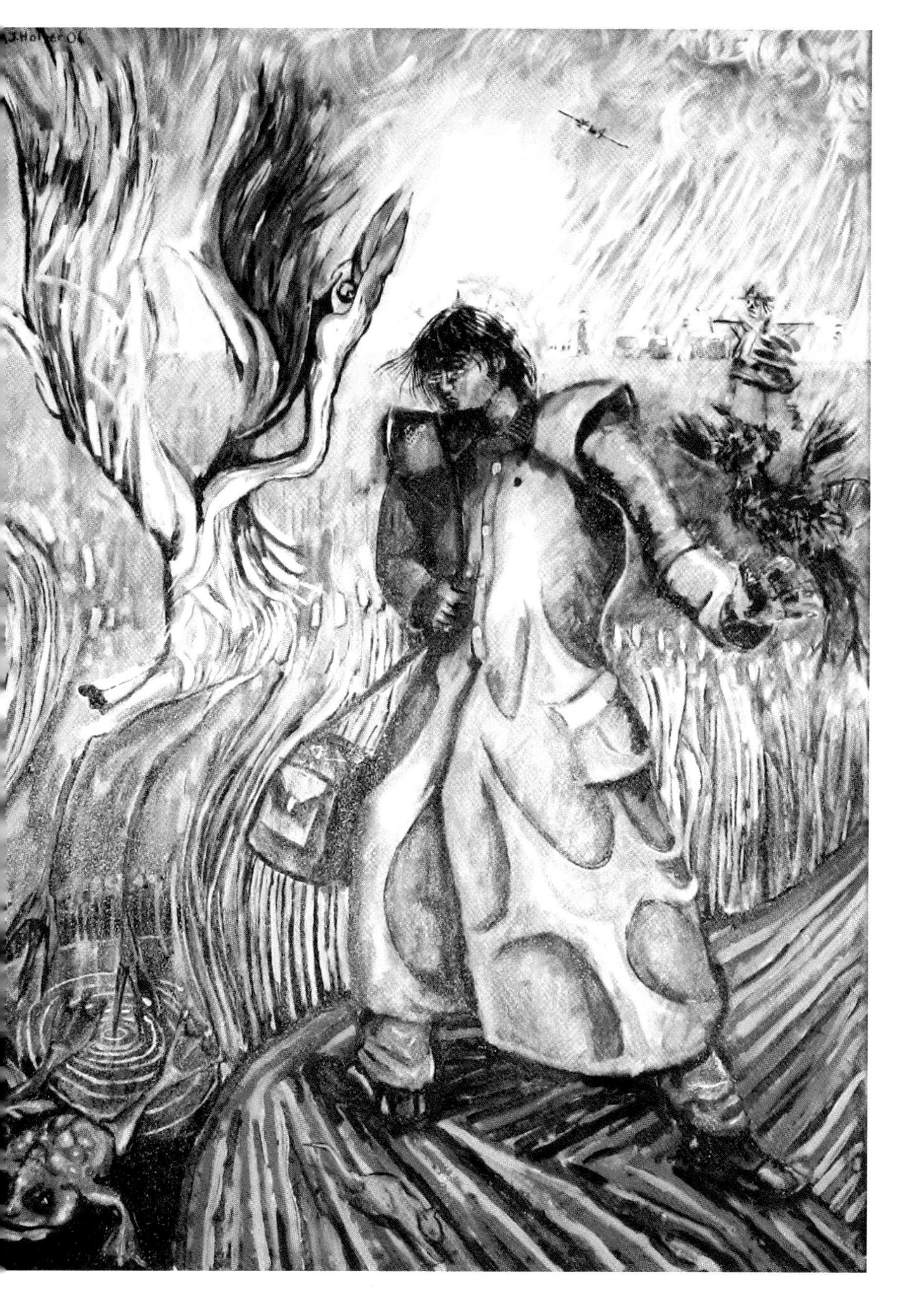

the prosperous town of Old Romney until one of these floods, which caused the course of the river to move nearly 2 miles to the north. Undeterred, the locals rebuilt the town on the new course of the river, enjoying the many benefits that having a sheltered sea port brought. The iron rings that ships tied up to can still be seen on the walls of the church in New Romney.

Unfortunately a much more devastating event was to occur. In 1287 a great storm not only diverted the course of the river Rother by 20 miles to Rye, it also flooded the whole town to a level of several feet for many days; the height of the flood water can still be seen by the stains on the church walls. The storm also brought devastation in the form of hundreds of thousands of tons of shingle which was washed into the town, destroying most of the buildings as well as covering the roads and fields in several feet of immovable stone. Even with the mechanical help that we enjoy today such an event would be devastating, and seven hundred years ago it caused the prosperous town of some 8000 inhabitants to dwindle to a few hundred peasants. Most of the houses were not rebuilt as they were buried under several feet of stone. The shingle is virtually impossible to dig out by hand, so even the church was left entombed in gravel – which is why you have to climb down several steps into it today.

At least Romney and Lydd escaped the fate of nearby Broomhill and Old Winchelsea, which were completely engulfed and destroyed by the tempests.

The relative isolation and inaccessibility of Dungeness, along with the unique environment, has resulted in a wide variety of unusual plants and animals crammed into this relatively small area. The importance of this area was recognised as far back as 1931 when Dungeness became the RSPB's first nature reserve; more recently the whole 12 square miles of Dungeness has become a national nature reserve. Most of the area, including privately owned land, has SSSI (Site of Special Scientific Interest) protection, which theoretically means you can be fined £2000 for picking even a blade of grass!

Despite the abundance of wildlife, Dungeness remains the only designated desert in mainland Europe.

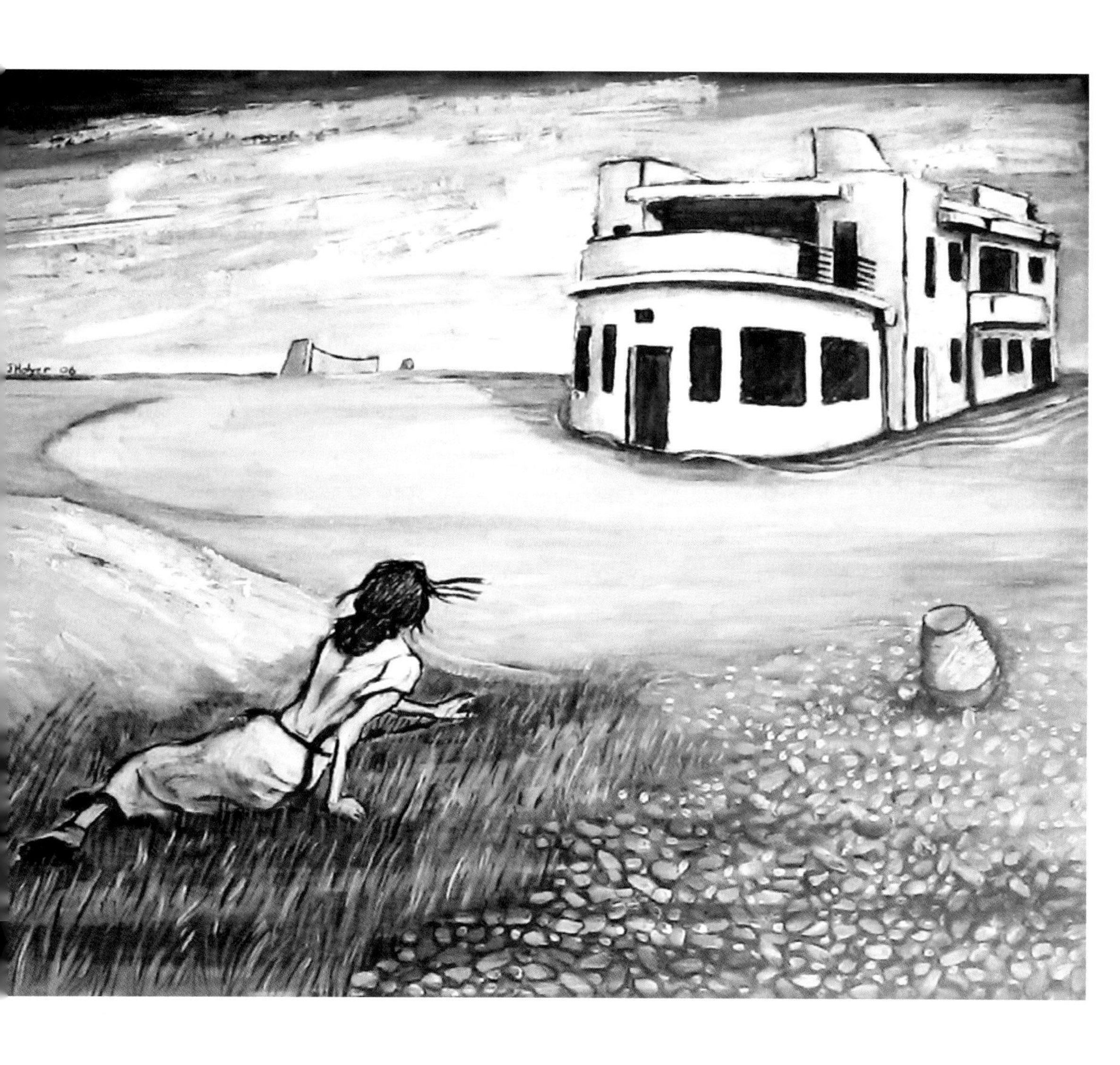

NANNY GOATS AND NAZIS

The isolation of Dungeness has not only encouraged and fostered but protected smuggling and other illegal activities over the years. The off the beaten track situation and somewhat mysterious reputation kept most people away and allowed a whole range of unusual practices and customs to develop, some of which persist to this day.

As with many isolated locations with difficult and dangerous access, Dungeness had and to some extent still has a very healthy barter economy. Most of the locals not only fished, but also kept goats for fresh milk, which roamed the shingle eating everything in their path – so much so that the area was locally known as Nanny Goat Island until recently. The area was also grazed by flocks of Lydd sheep within living memory. Both sets of ruminants helped to keep the shingle bare of all but the hardiest vegetation, allowing the area to evolve some of the unique flora and fauna it now boasts. Paradoxically, since the area has become more and more protected grasses have taken root. It is said that very soon they will have carpeted nearly all of the shingle, strangling out most of the unique plants and animals that are supposed to be protected.

Such isolation meant that there was much more emphasis on self sufficiency and recycling, which still lives on in the descendants of the original inhabitants. The nearest shops were in Lydd, which is a difficult 6 mile round trip over shingle. A trip to the shops there was a major event and certainly not something that locals would have done as a matter of course. Even a short journey across shingle can be difficult, especially when carrying something. For this reason locals evolved a form of footwear known as a backstay (or baxter); these were flat wooden boards worn under the shoe, fastened over with a leather strap and used something like a snow shoe. These backstays were used well into the 1980s by some of the older residents, and examples can still be seen at the Pilot Inn and the Lydd museum.

Although life must have been hard most of the time, there was still time for enjoyment and socialising. Dungeness evolved its own form of blackfaced morris dancing, which carried on as late as the 1950s. This unusual mutation of the English folk tradition was performed by a group of local men who blackened their faces and travelled round the community, entertaining at each household, playing instruments and dancing. It is difficult to trace the roots of

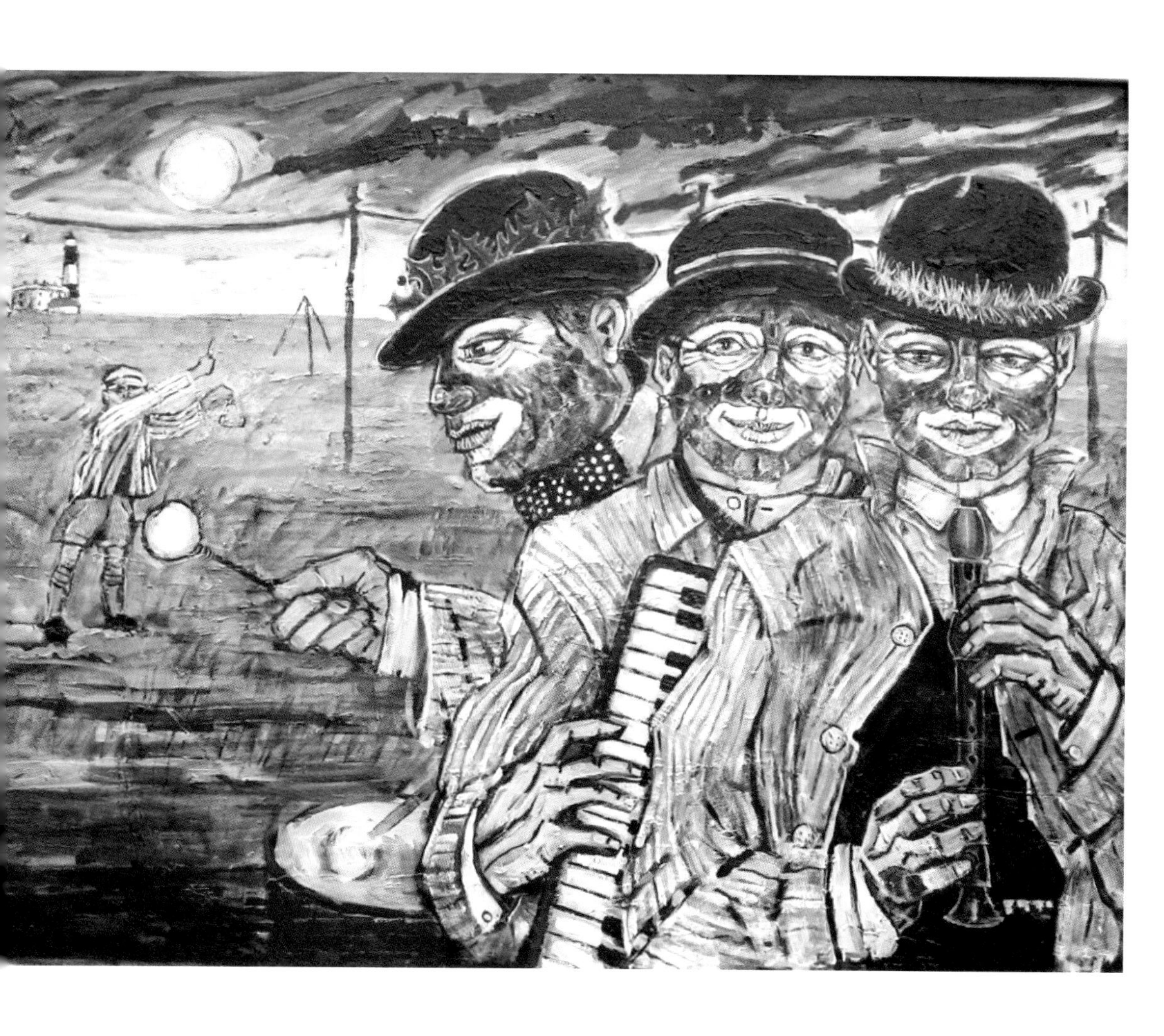

this activity, but the community has a tradition of absorbing many of the unfortunate people who were shipwrecked on its shores; these newcomers would not only have brought their own traditions, but they would have been a welcome addition to the rather limited gene pool. One of the oldest families on Dungeness (the Richardsons) descends from Huguenot refugees who arrived in the eighteenth century from France. To this day the eldest son in the family carries the middle name of Twosign, a Black African shipwrecked in the nineteenth century who lived out the rest of his life in Lydd, marrying a Richardson and adopting the name.

Even the pubs of Dungeness are unusual. Until the advent of roads, which were built during the Second World War, most of the pubs' trade came via the sea. The Hope and Anchor, which is now buried under a nuclear reactor, had virtually no habitation nearby, had no road to it and was well known as a fisherman's pub. Deliveries of heavy beer barrels to the pubs must have been very difficult over the shingle; not only did the horses wear their own version of backstays, but a special cart with large drum-like wooden wheels was used until the advent of roads. This unique conveyance can still be seen in Lydd museum.

The isolated nature of the area and the relative ease of ring fencing it for protection were instrumental in the building of Lydd barracks and ranges, which have been on the same site since 1881. This important military installation has been instrumental in both world wars and is heavily relied upon to this day. Many important military developments were conceived, tried and tested in Lydd. One of the first, in the late nineteenth century, was Lyddite – which was a forerunner of dynamite. In 1908 US showman Samuel F. Cody (he falsely clamed to be the son of Buffalo Bill Cody but was the first man to fly in Britain) was resident in Lydd; he helped to develop and fly the first manned observation kites from the site. During the First World War tanks were developed and tested on the site. The 1920s saw the development and testing of listening ears (acoustic sound mirrors). During the Second World War the whole of the Dungeness peninsula was requisitioned by the MOD and heavily fortified, being totally cut off from the rest of the country. Locals were only allowed out or back in after onerous security checks.

On 3 September 1940 four German spies landed somewhere between Hythe and Dungeness, but owing to their apparent stupidity and the fact that they stood out so much in such an isolated and tight-knit area they were caught virtually immediately, especially as only one of them was able to speak English. One spy was arrested in a local pub, the Rising Sun, at 9.30 am, because he wanted to buy a drink, and locals would have known the pub did not open until 10 am. This suspicious behaviour tipped off a local RAF officer, and when the visitor failed to produce the required permit that would have allowed him to travel freely along the coastline he was handed over to the police. Another of the four was caught; it was discovered he had hidden radio equipment in a tree not far from the Lydd to Dungeness road. They were all tried and sentenced to death by hanging.

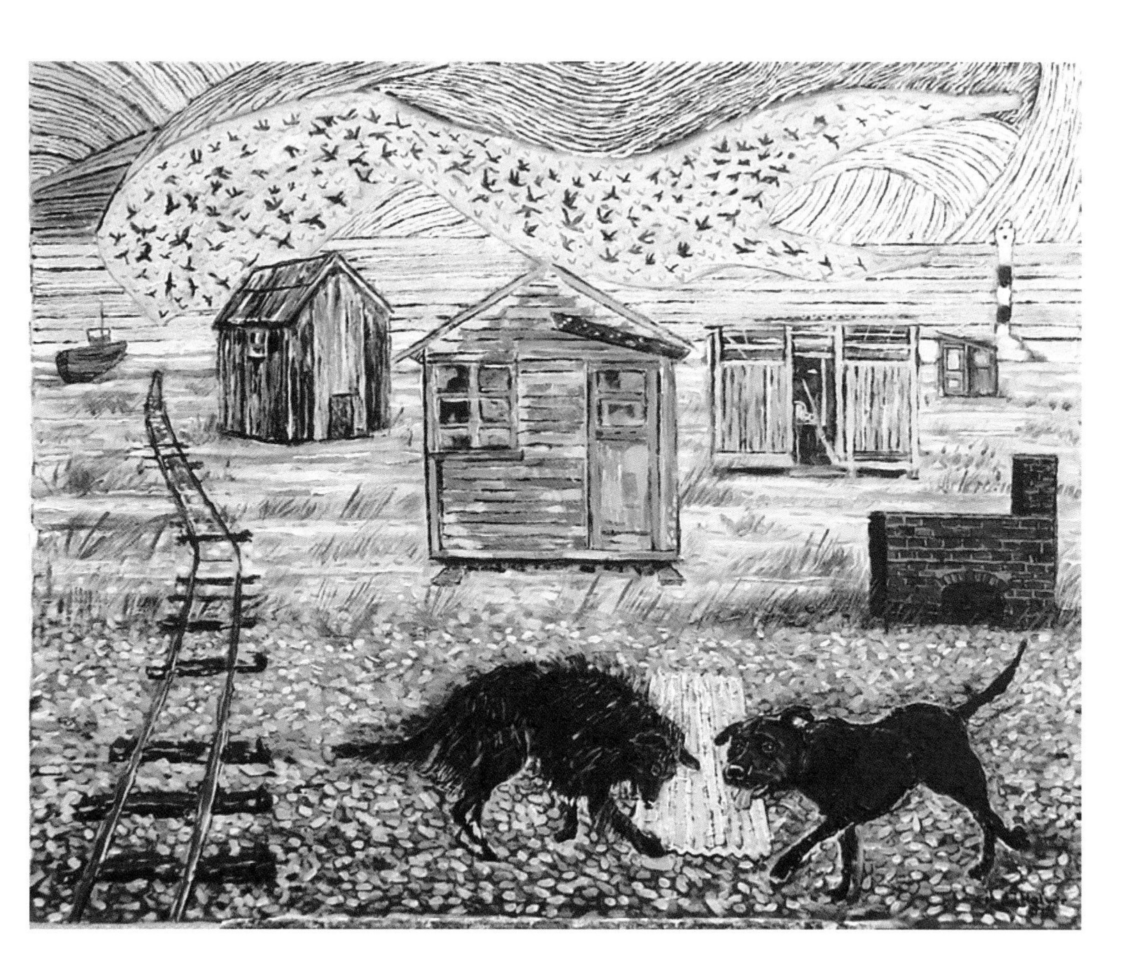

A PRETTY KETTLE OF FISH

Today it is common to observe rows of self-absorbed and anoraked anglers sitting like sentinels on shingle along the coast, wistfully wishing for a codling. These are the spiritual descendants of a once thriving fishing community that led a harsh existence here, clinging to these beaches in hope of a profitable catch.

Herring fishing was the 'gold standard' of the local economy right back to the medieval period, when salted herring was traded from the Cinque Ports at the annual fair at Great Yarmouth. Remains of 'herring hangs' (towers for smoking fish) can still be seen in Lydd and Dungeness. The painting depicts Jim Moate, for many years a well-known local character who specialised in traditional smoking methods.

Along the coast are dotted net boiling ketches. These look like large laundry ovens, complete with chimneys and copper bowls, used to infuse nets with a tar solution to protect against the salt water.

In its heyday the fishing industry of Dungeness was serviced by a standard gauge railway service to Billingsgate. Remains of this railway, the narrow gauge railways from the beach to the road and railheads can still be seen today.

Besides drift netting Romney fishermen used a couple of techniques, now abandoned, that are worth recording. The first was seine netting, whereby a rowing boat would go out in the path of an approaching shoal, drop a net screen, then furiously paddle back inshore behind the shoal to trap the fish.

The second was kettle netting, which used a form of trapnet. Poles and netting were placed in the beach at low tide. A funnel net led the shoal into the trap of a circular enclosure which was emptied at the next low tide. The furious and frustrated attempts of the fish to escape caused the water to 'boil', hence 'a pretty kettle of fish'.

Despite changing economic and technical times, professional fishing clings on tenaciously. Indeed, the largest fishing vessel in its history is soon to be launched off the beach at Dungeness. Substantial local catches of fish are still landed and enjoyed by locals and visitors alike.

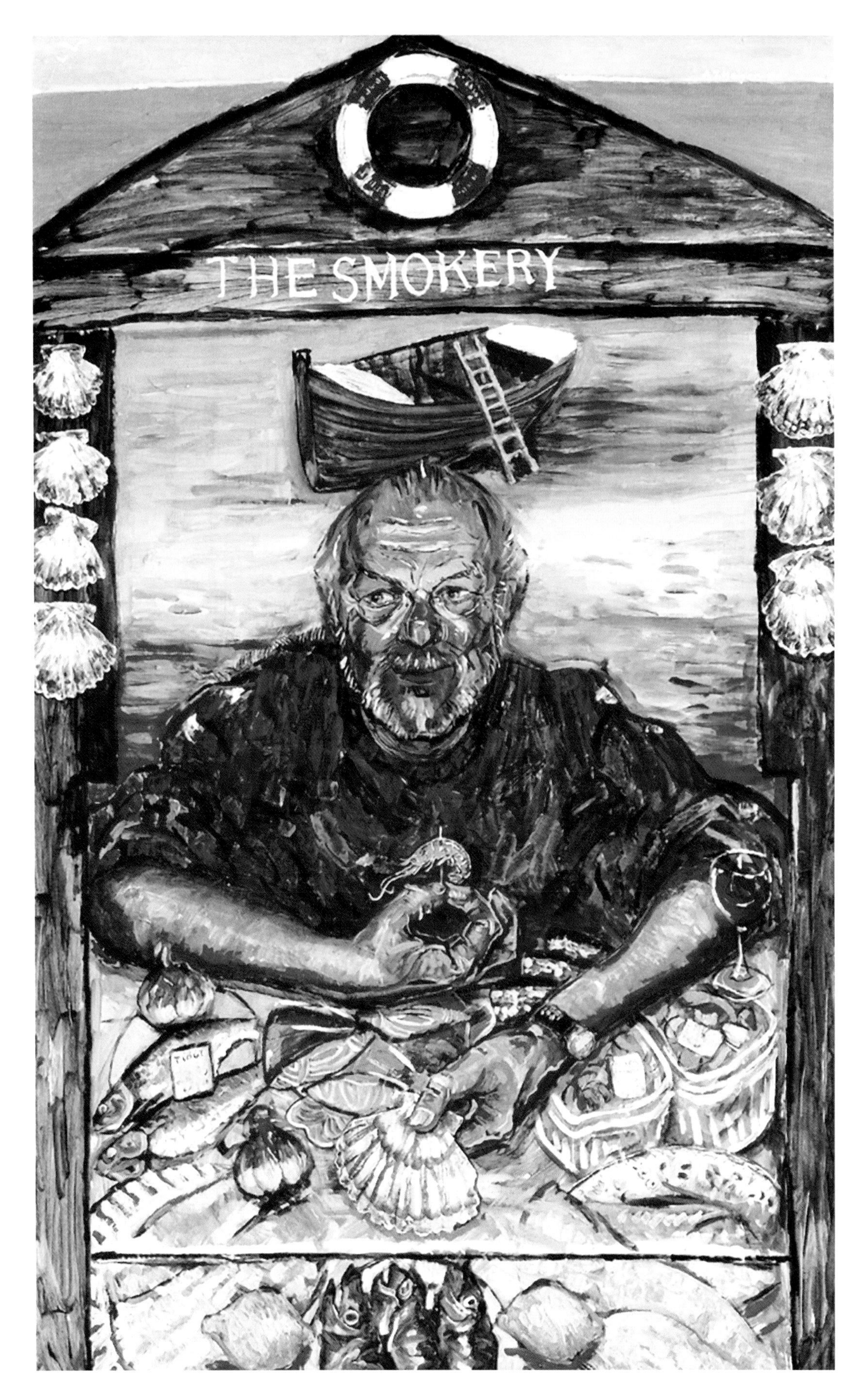
THE SMOKERY

THE LIFEBOAT AND LADY LAUNCHERS

The Dungeness lifeboat has a long and distinguished history, being on one of the busiest shipping routes in the world until the advent of shipping lanes and modern navigational methods. It was one of the most used lifeboats in Britain.

Most lifeboats in Britain have a slipway that allows them to be launched at any stage of the tide. The constantly shifting shingle at Dungeness does not allow this so, like the fishing fleet, the lifeboat had to be launched by being pulled over lengths of hard wood placed at intervals on the shingle. These 'woods', as they are known, are 8 foot lengths of oak or ash, with ropes attached so they can be pulled out after the boat has passed over them and be quickly run round to the front of the boat to be reused in its journey to or back from the sea.

This method of launching is still used by the local fishing boats today. In addition to this laborious task the lifeboat had to be pulled from and back into its shelter. The local tradition of women being responsible for the backbreaking and dangerous task of launching the lifeboat and the fishing boats is not, as it may seem, a misogynistic one. They traditionally did this job in order to make sure that the men stayed dry; to get wet before going out in an exposed boat in winter was hazardous in the extreme, and could even result in death. For that reason, not only were the boats launched by women but in rough seas women would carry their men to the boats to prevent them from getting wet. Women launched and retrieved the lifeboat until surplus American tractors found their way to the Marsh in the 1950s. The lifeboat is now launched and retrieved by a custom-built tracked vehicle.

The first official lifeboat was sent to Dungeness in 1826, and six silver medals and two gold medals were awarded for gallantry between the 1830s and the 1850s. The Dungeness lifeboat, *Providence*, was moved to New Romney in 1861 and there was no direct protection for the very dangerous waters around the Point. Despite several terrible shipwrecks the lifeboats of Rye and Romney continued to cover this remote location. In 1873 a dreadful collision occurred just off Dungeness, when the ship *Northfleet* was lost. The public attention which this tragedy attracted, because of the heavy loss of life, resulted in the reopening of Dungeness Lifeboat Station in 1874. It also

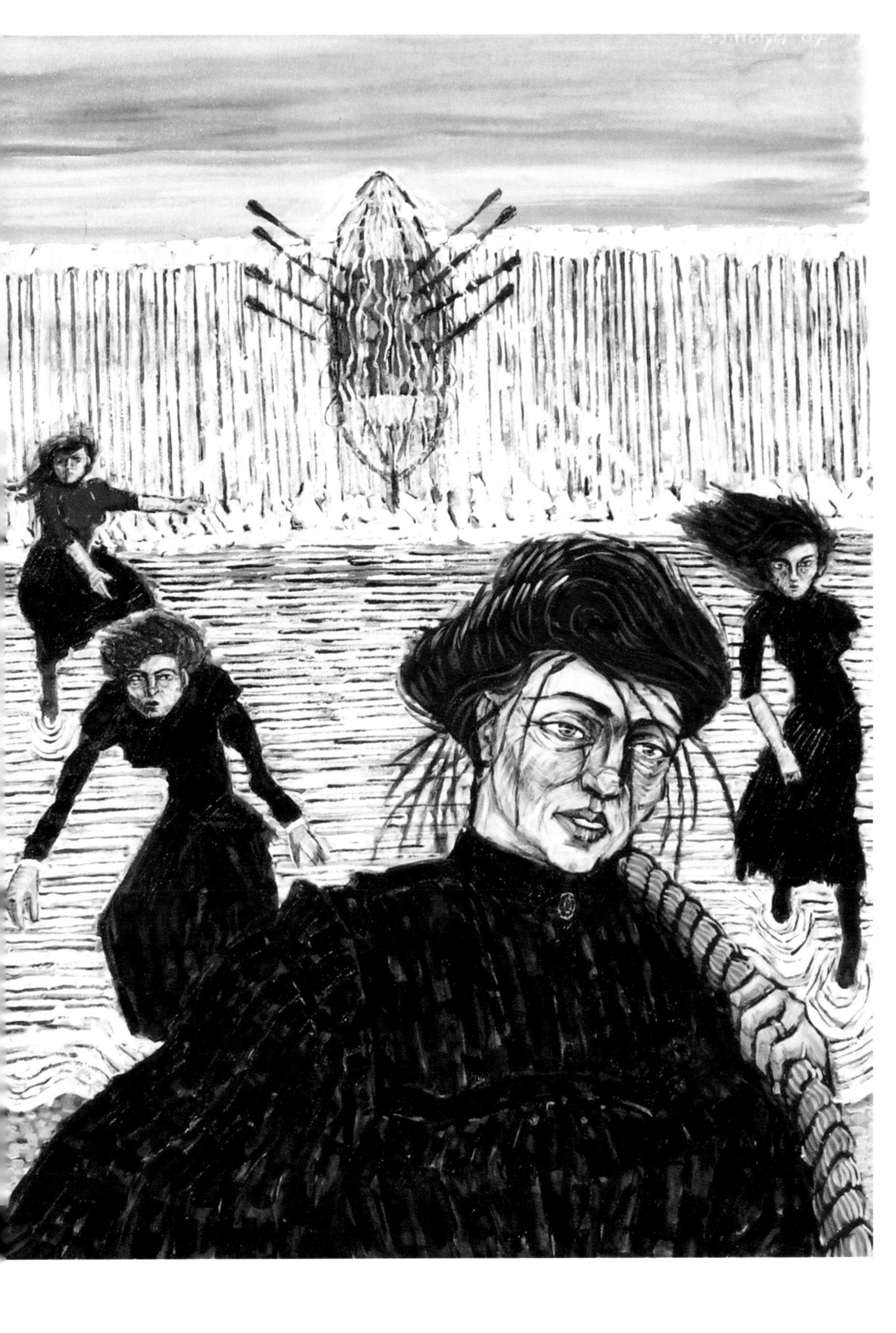

resulted in the first standardised emergency and distress systems in the world, most of which are still used today.

Most of the Dungeness lifeboats' distinguished history has been dominated by the three main families of Dungeness, the Tarts, the Oillers and the Richardsons; indeed in any crew list until very recently you would be pushed to find any other name. Andy Holyer's great grandfather, Charles Sharp, was coxswain of the Littlestone lifeboat in the early twentieth century, and his part in the rescue of the *Malpas Belle* is illustrated in the painting 'The Witches of Dungeness'.

The present boat is a Mersey class named *Pride and Spirit*; it arrived in 1992. Thanks to the advent of radio, radar and more recently Channel shipping lanes, shipping in the Channel and around Dungeness Point is now safer, and the Dungeness lifeboat station is now much less busy.

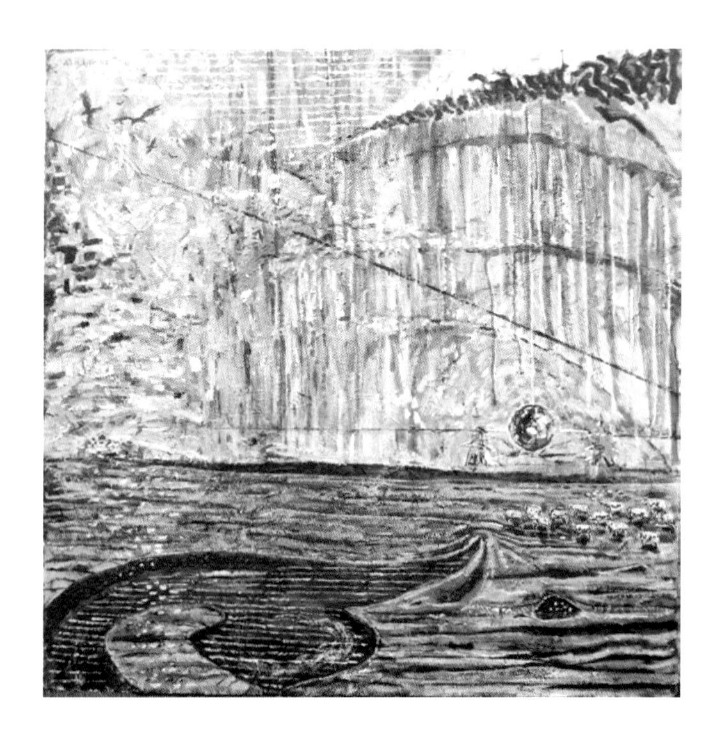

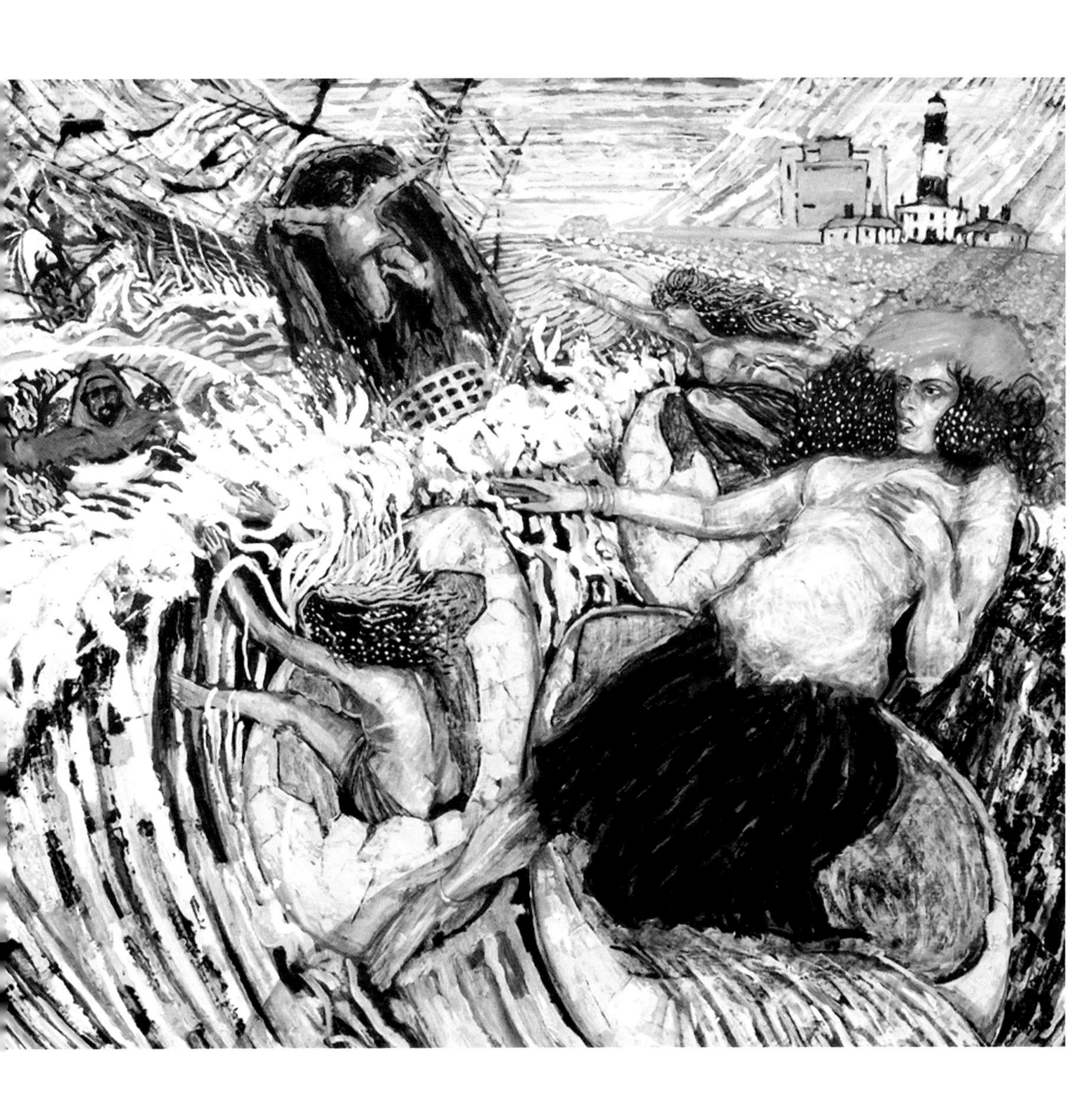

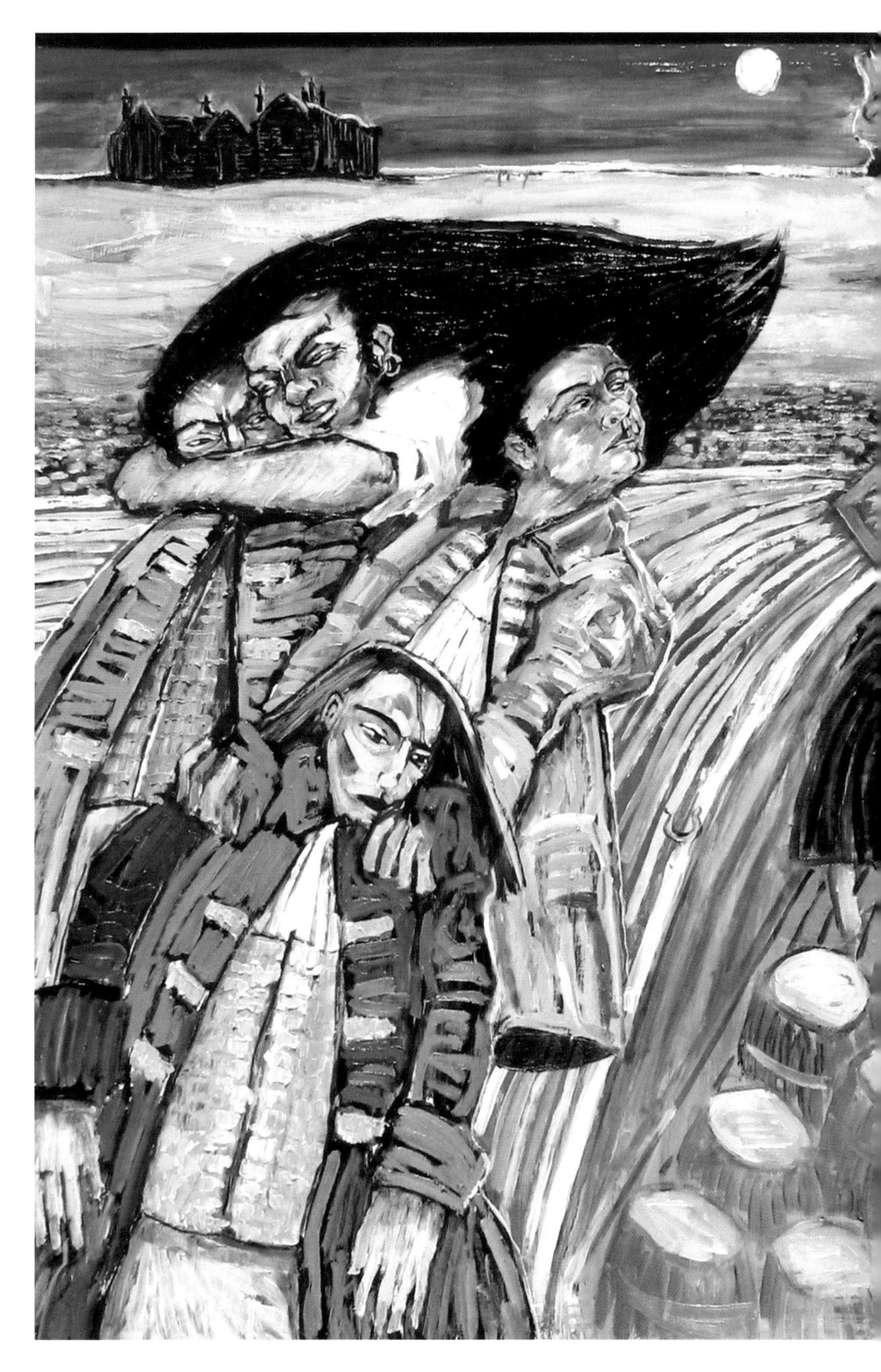

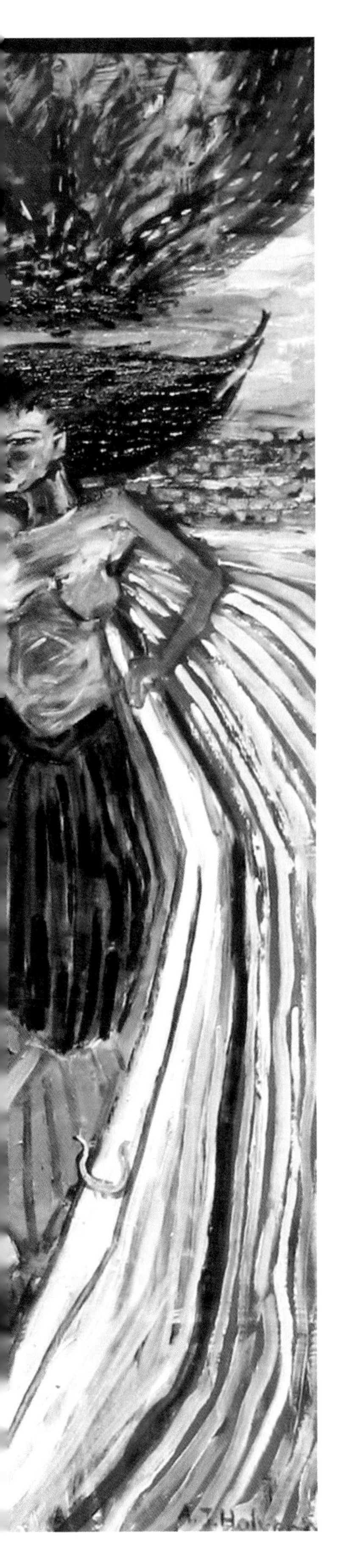

OWLERS, SCARECROWS AND WITCHES IN EGGSHELLS

Dungeness and Romney Marsh have a long tradition of mystery, hauntings and supernatural goings on. To a large extent the area was a no-go area for much of the last couple of thousand years. Although the area was largely inaccessible because of its geography and topography, not to mention its reputation for being a very unhealthy environment (the Marsh was the last place where malaria was endemic in Britain and it was only eradicated in the early twentieth century), a large part of its unwelcoming reputation was deliberately cultivated by the local population, including its upper classes. It would have been virtually impossible for a high volume of contraband to be processed through the area without the involvement or compliance of nearly everybody resident there. This deliberate isolation was essential for the wide range of illicit goings on, which needed to be carried out in secrecy so there was as little risk as possible (even the penalty for wool smuggling was death).The area was considered so ungovernable by the Crown that it boasted its own currency and parliament until well into the nineteenth century.

The Dr Syn novels of Russell Thorndike, with his strong images of smugglers disguised as spectral scarecrows, are fictional but are woven around the whole aura of mystery and secrecy that the area has cultivated right up to the present day. The Reverend Richard Barham, writing in 1793, described the area thus: "The world, according to the best geographers, is divided into Europe, Asia, Africa, America, and Romney Marsh. In this last-named, and fifth, quarter of the globe, a witch may still be occasionally discovered in favourable, i.e., stormy, seasons, weathering Dungeness Point in an eggshell, or careering on her broomstick over Dymchurch Wall." It's easy to see the value of these local demons in deterring unwanted attention and leaving the citizenry to continue their nefarious activities unimpeded.

Although the smugglers have acquired a romantic image over time, in many ways becoming a modern version of the tales of Robin Hood and his band of merry outlaws, there is no doubt that their heyday was a brutal and unforgiving time. The rewards were high but the consequence of being caught was usually death. Battles with the law enforcers were frequent and often resulted in many dead and injured. The penalty for anyone foolish enough to inform or be indiscreet was swift and brutal.

The graves of six excise men killed in a battle with local smugglers lie near the Pilot Inn, and many more casualties of the smuggling wars are interred in Lydd graveyard.

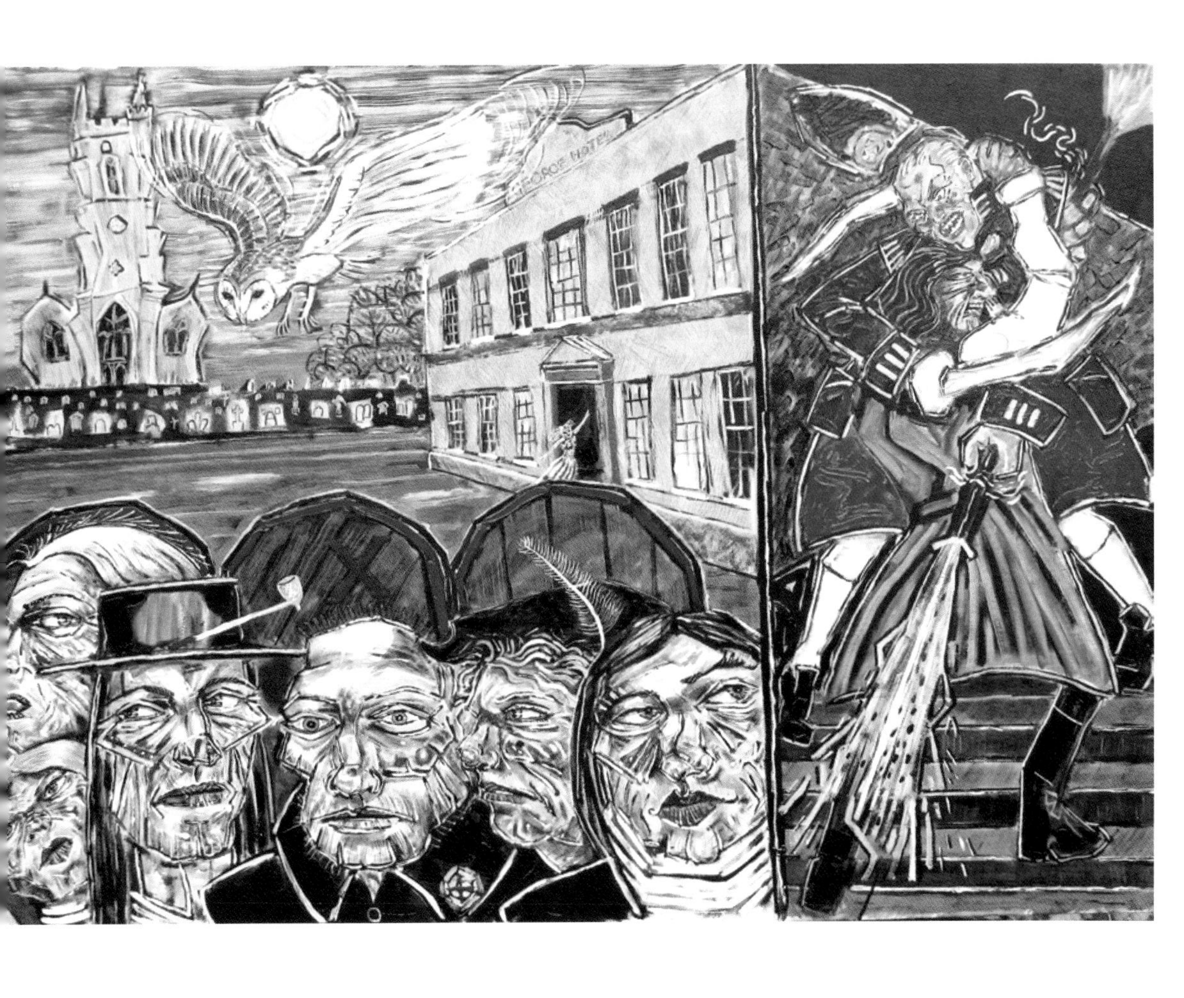

LYDD: ON THE ROAD TO NOWHERE

Today Lydd retains its charm because of its sense of isolation. There are no main roads, no supermarkets, no ring roads, no burger bars, no industrial estates. It sits quietly on the road to nowhere, and is content. However, this was not always the case.

Lydd reached the height of its prosperity during the thirteenth century, when it was a corporate member of the Cinque Ports, a 'limb' of Romney. In 1287 a great storm moved the mouth of the River Rother some 10 miles to the west to Rye; this resulted in Lydd no longer having proper access to the sea.

The focal point of Lydd (and some say the whole of Romney Marsh) is the medieval All Saints' Church, aka 'The Cathedral of the Marsh'. At 199 feet it is the longest church in Kent. Its main feature is a fifteenth-century tower, which at 132 feet is one of the tallest in Kent; it features four asymmetrical spires. During the Middle Ages the church featured several altars along with ten candle-lit shrines. At the north-west corner of the nave is all that remains of the much older stone Saxon church, which dates to before 740 AD. The church was long thought to be Saxon in origin, but recent studies have dated the oldest section to the latter half of the fifth century, making it Romano-British. Local folklore says that the church was originally dedicated to the brother Saints Crispin and Crispinian.

In 1940 the chancel of the church was destroyed by a direct hit from a bomb; the
sanctuary was destroyed and the roofs and windows badly damaged. The organist was playing the organ at the time and had a miraculous escape, as did his two helpers who were pumping the organ bellows, not to mention the two soldiers on watch at the top of the tower. Further attacks in 1944 caused even more damage. When the war was over and sufficient funds were raised a painstaking reconstruction and restoration was undertaken using the original materials. This was finally completed in 1958. There are a disproportionate number of sailors buried in the churchyard because of the huge attrition rate in the stormy and dangerous seas which surround the town.

In addition there is the grave of Captain Edgar, who accompanied Captain Cook on some of his most significant voyages. Indeed, he witnessed Cook's murder in Hawaii.

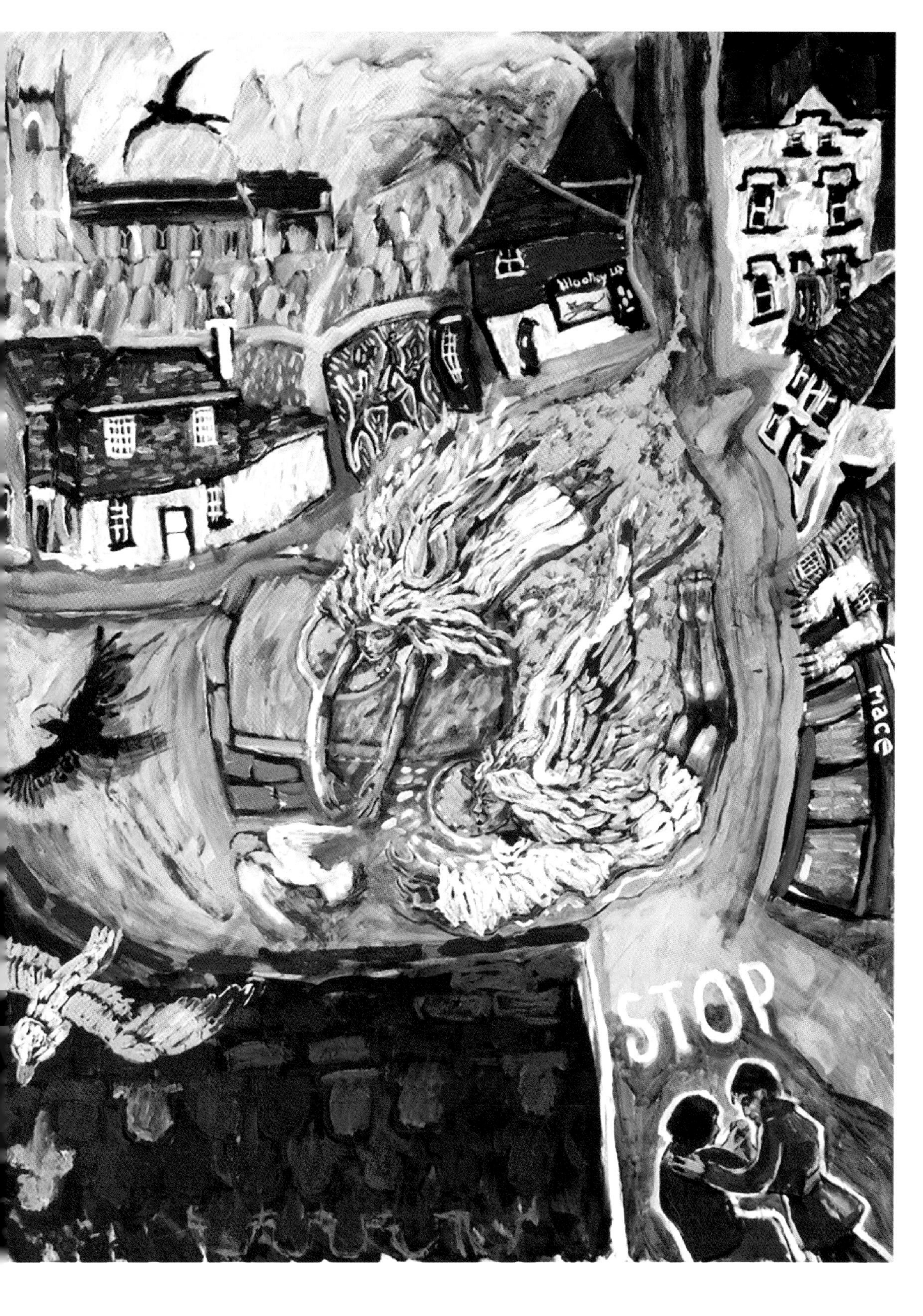
mace
STOP

As you would expect, because of its location Lydd was a magnet for smugglers or "owlers". In 1717, two memebers of the Myafield Gang were temporarily imprisoned at the George Inn after being captured at Dungeness; they were guarded by six men with loaded flintlocks. Undeterred, nine locals rushed into the George firing their weapons, while outside over 100 more local people waited in case help was needed. Needless to say the smugglers escaped.

In the 1820s, as the anti-smuggling efforts around Dymchurch started to take effect, the infamous Aldington gang moved to the safer confines of Lydd. They wasted no time in asserting themselves, quickly crushing (or buying) the small amount of authority that existed there. At this time the owlers considered themselves so untouchable that in 1829 they paraded a convoy of smuggled goods through the middle of Lydd in broad daylight, to the delight of cheering crowds. Many of the houses in Lydd are deliberately and sometimes secretly linked through their roof spaces; this allowed easy access and escape for smugglers.

Before the First World War Lydd became an important artillery practice camp. Experiments with high explosives carried out on the shingle wastes around 1888 led to the invention of the explosive Lyddite. Lydd was at one time a garrison town, and the area is still an important training ground for the military. Inhabitants regularly awake and fall asleep to the sound of gunfire.

Lydd airport, or Ferryfield, was the first civil airport to be constructed in Britain after the Second World War; it is now known as London Ashford airport. Lydd airport (or Fairfield airport as it was then known) became the busiest post-war passenger airport in Britain. It mainly catered for the wealthy who transported their sports cars and selves over the Channel, heading for the South of France. Silver City was the main carrier with its fleet of Bristol freighters. Today it is proposed to re-establish Lydd as a major airport.

An amazing event occurred on 27 November 1940. A railway train that was just leaving Lydd station came under attack from two German Focke-Wulf 190s. The train was hit and its boiler exploded. The debris from the exploding engine hit one of the planes, causing it to crash nearby and killing the pilot. The fireman on the railway engine was injured. This was the only example of a locomotive 'kill' during the Battle of Britain.

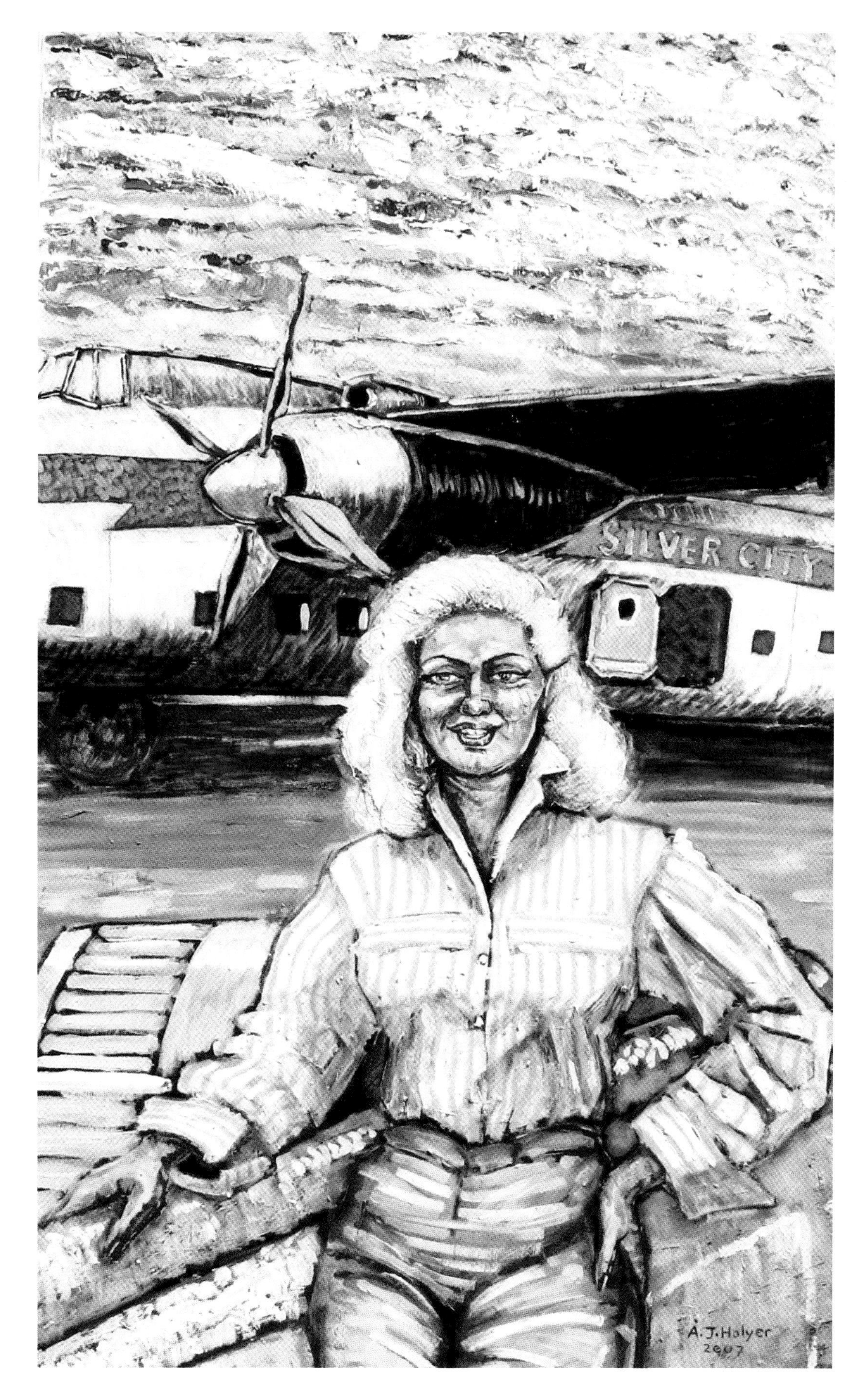
SILVER CITY
A.J.Holyer
2007

Lydd was home to the Sun Brewery, later to become Edwin Finn and Sons. The brewery is famous for having exploiting the process invented by Joseph Priestley to carbonate water (adding fizzy bubbles). By the mid-nineteenth century the brewery was doing a roaring trade in fizzy pop and was one of the largest users of Codd bottles (the ones with the glass marble stopper) in the country. In so doing they gave us the expression 'codswallop'.

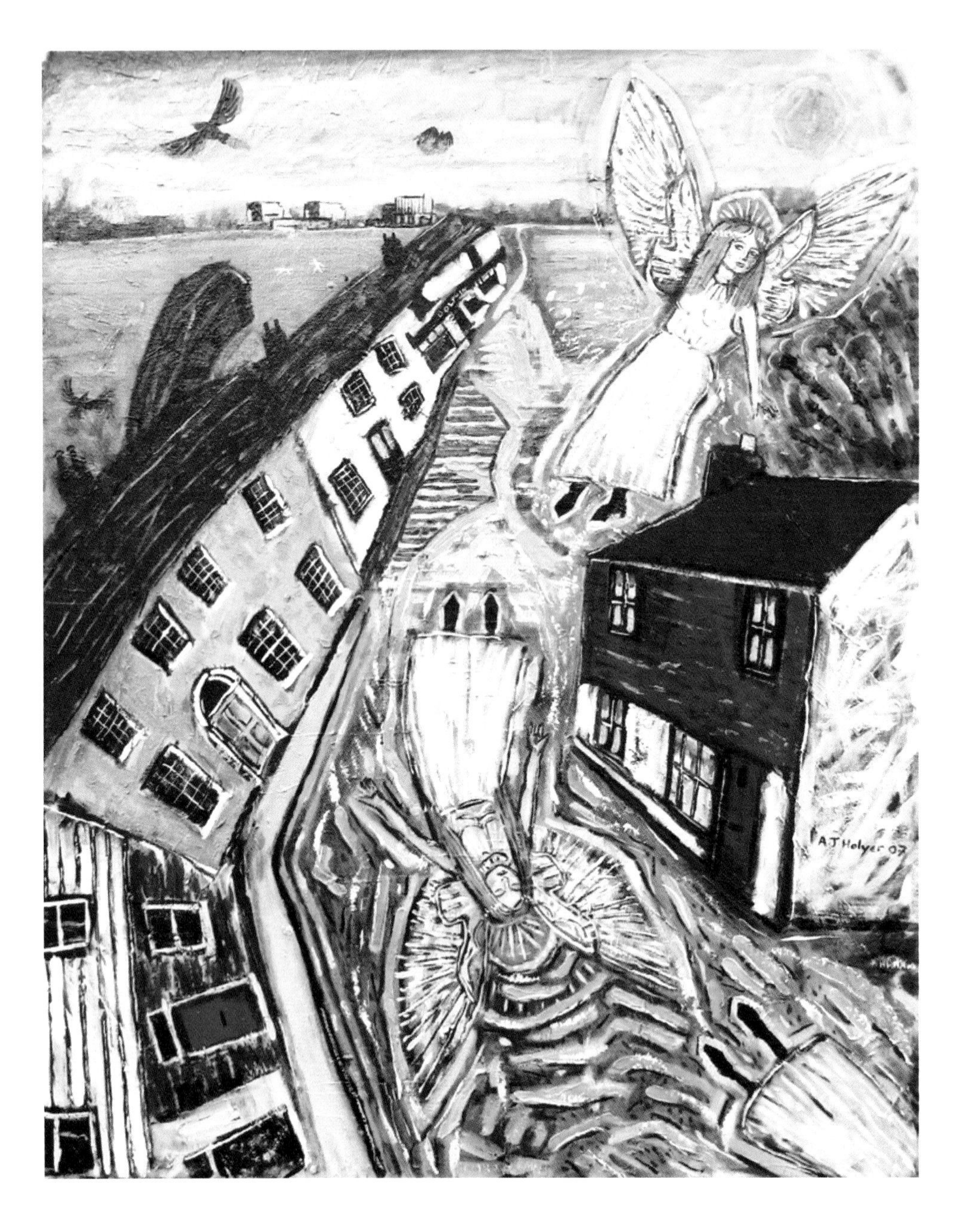

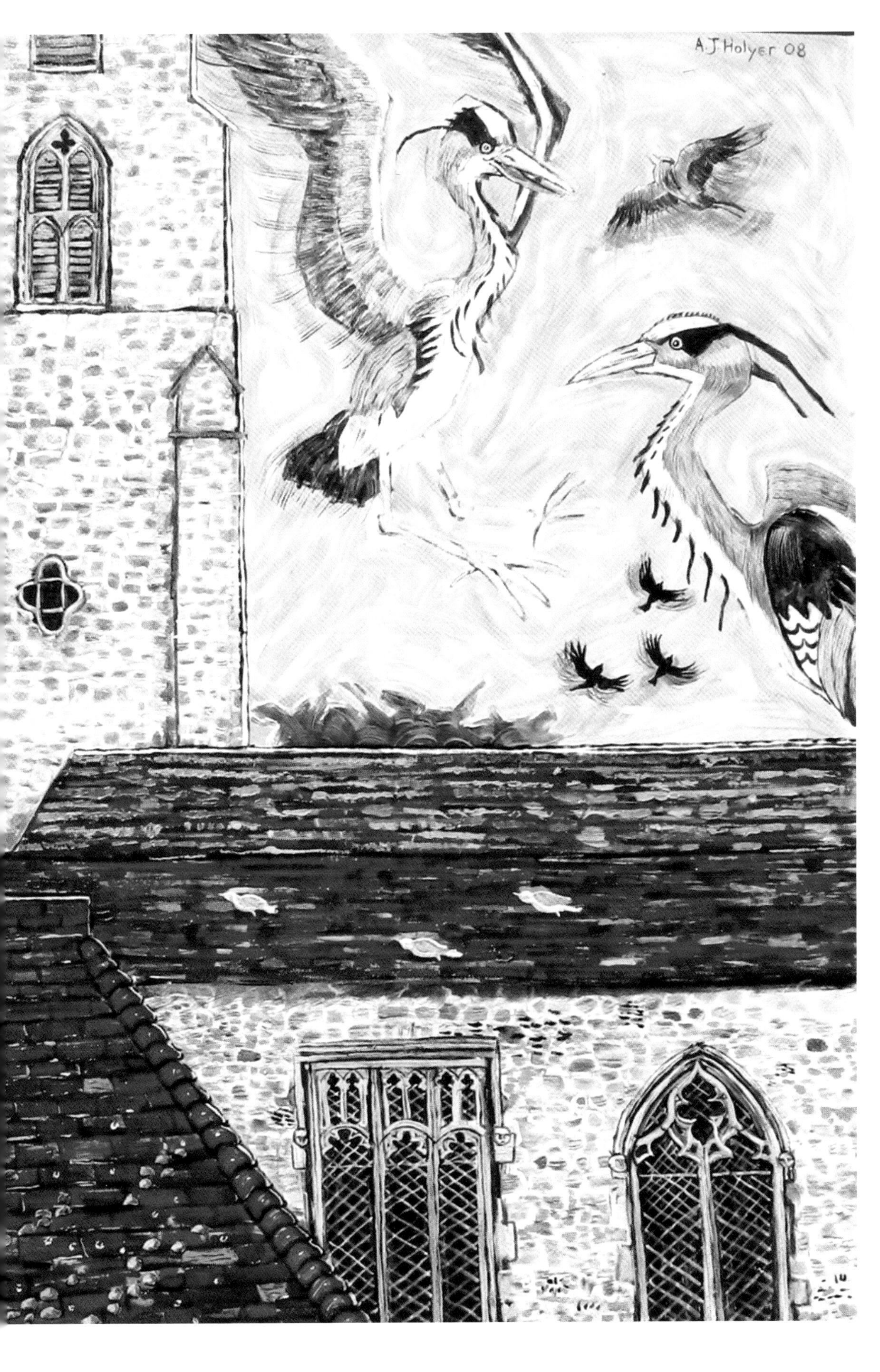
A.J. Holyer 08

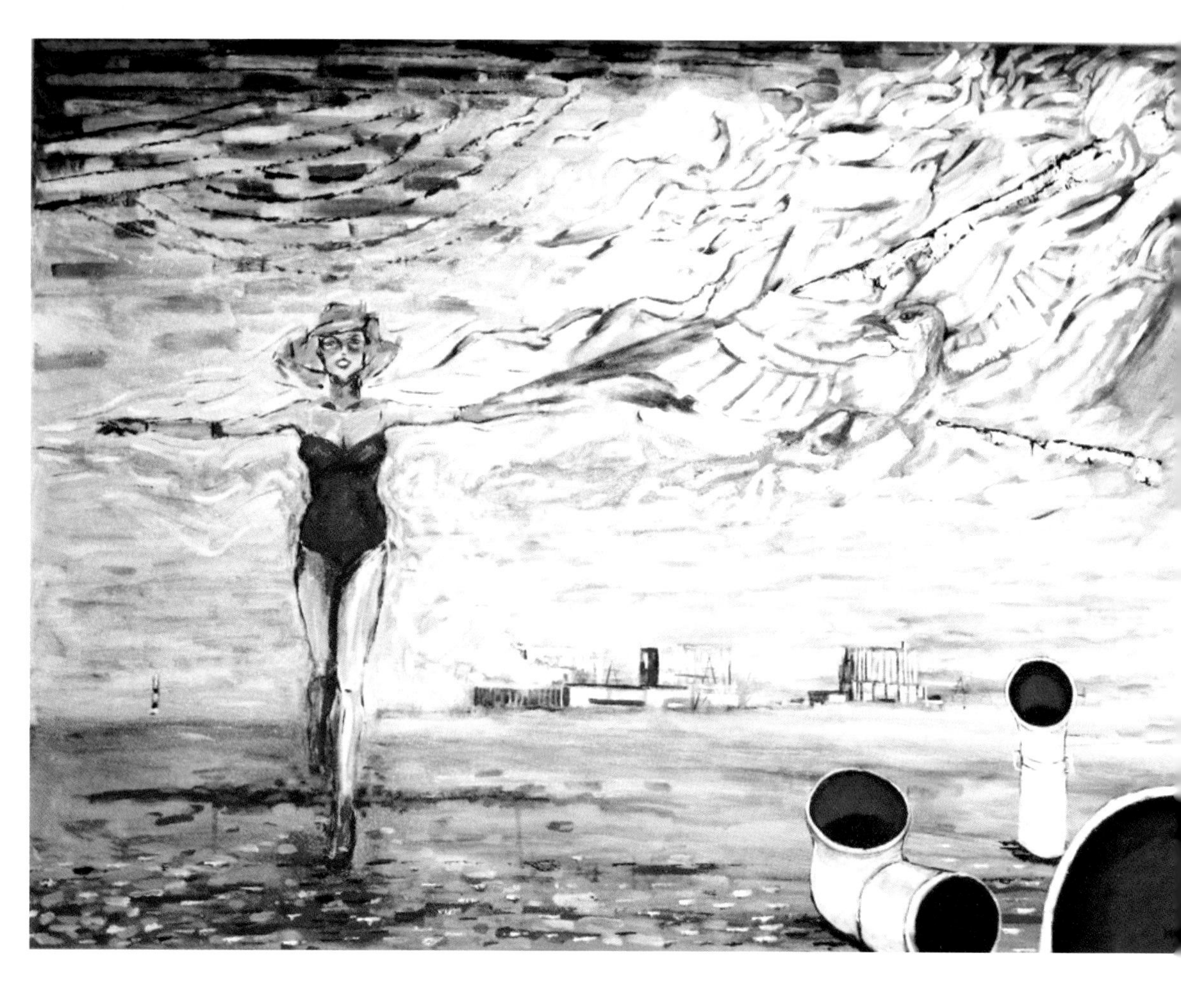

DUNGENESS POWER STATIONS

The huge monoliths that are the buildings of Dungeness A and B power stations stand like sentinels guarding the whole of Romney Marsh. From Dover, looking south towards the Marsh, Dungeness power station appears like a vast ship floating in the sea. This is because the curvature of the earth causes the low-lying marsh to disappear over the horizon, leaving only the massive reactor buildings in view.

Dungeness power station consists of two nuclear reactors. The first, A station, was connected to the national grid in 1965. It is of the obsolete but reliable Magnox gas cooled design and could be used to generate power and to make plutonium for nuclear weapons. It had a generating output of nearly 500 megawatts or half a gigawatt. The station reached the end of its designed operating life in 2006 and is in the process of being dismantled and decontaminated. It is thought that this will take about a hundred years.

although there is an alternative more aggressive plan that could see the process completed in twenty-five years.

B station is an AGR or advanced gas cooled reactor. It was switched on in 1983 and produces 1200 megawatts or 1.2 gigawatts. B station is due to be closed in 2018.

Both stations are built on the largest area of open shingle in Europe and possibly the world. Over thousands of years Dungeness has been built up by the deposit of shingle scoured from the whole of the south coast of England, in a process known as long shore drift. Over the years the whole mass of shingle has not only been increasing but has been moving slowly north and east, as the sea moves the shingle from one side of the Ness to the other. The effect of this can easily be seen by looking at the traditional fishermen's houses, all of which would have been built close to the east coast of the Ness but are now stranded some half a mile inland. Even the current version of The Pilot, built on the beach in the late '50s, is now some 150 yards inland. After the power stations were built it was quickly realised that unless something was done the shingle bank would soon be eroded away and the reactors would be underwater. A fleet of lorries is used 365 days a year to transport shingle from the east side of the Ness back to the other side of the power station in order to maintain the shingle sea defences for the plant. It is estimated that coastal erosion would otherwise move shingle at an estimated rate of 6 yards per year, quickly swamping the power stations. Around 30,000 cubic yards of shingle are moved each year. About 22 million gallons of cooling water are extracted and returned to the sea each hour. The cooling process heats the water by some 12° Celsius (22° F). This means that there is a vast amount of water often at a temperature of over 25° being pumped back into the sea. There are many local stories of fantastic fish and unusual creatures mutating in this veritable tropical paradise. The process of extracting water to cool the reactors also results in many fish being sucked into the system; these are normally filtered out in large screens, which are regularly cleared to reduce the risk of blockage. There are also stories of power station employees coming home with huge fish that have been caught on the screens, although nowadays it is not permitted to take any of the fish; they are all macerated in a huge mincer and dumped back at sea. On occasions the power stations have had to be closed because the huge volume of fish blocking the screens has restricted the reactor cooling water. There have even been instances where screens have been holed and seals have been sucked into the system.

When both power stations were working to full capacity they would have been producing some 1.7 gigawatts between them. This is enough to light nearly half a billion low energy household light bulbs. They would have easily powered the whole of Kent, and most of London too.

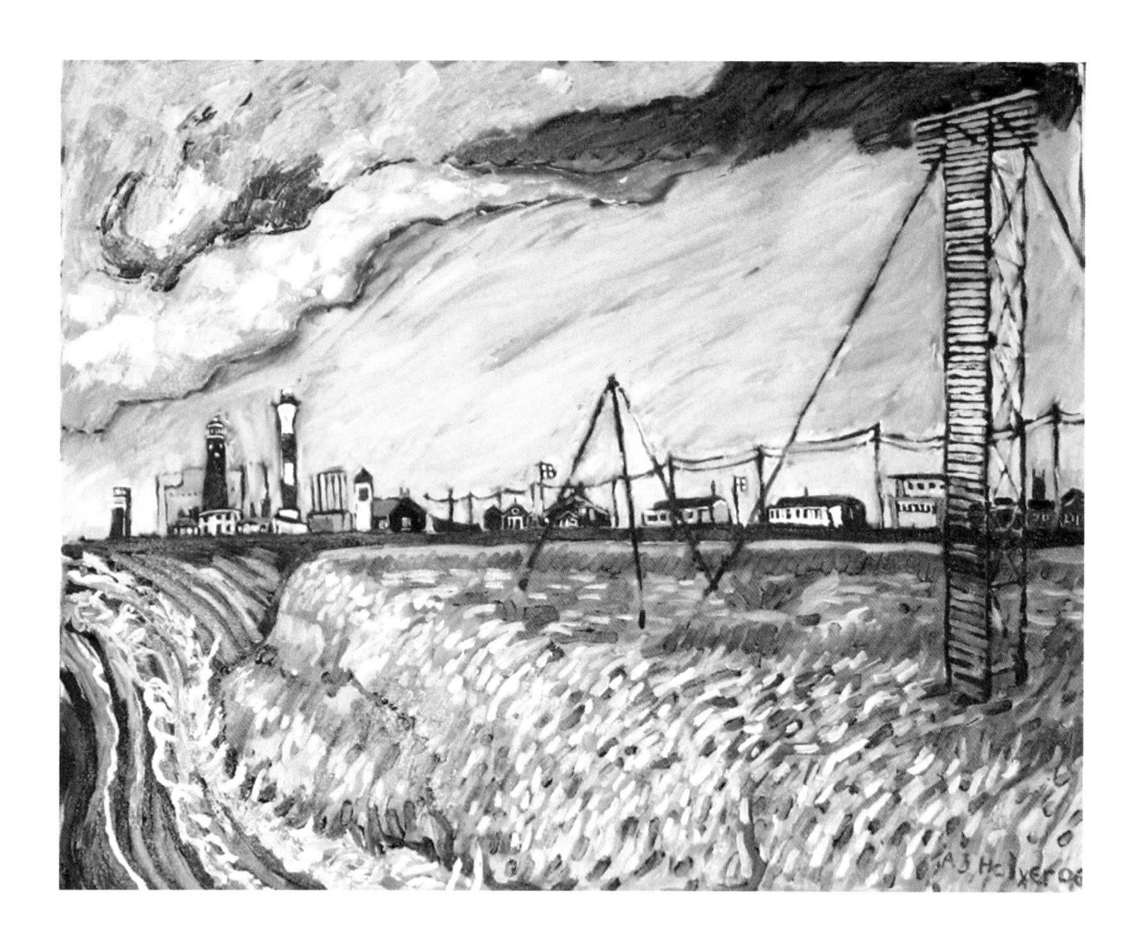

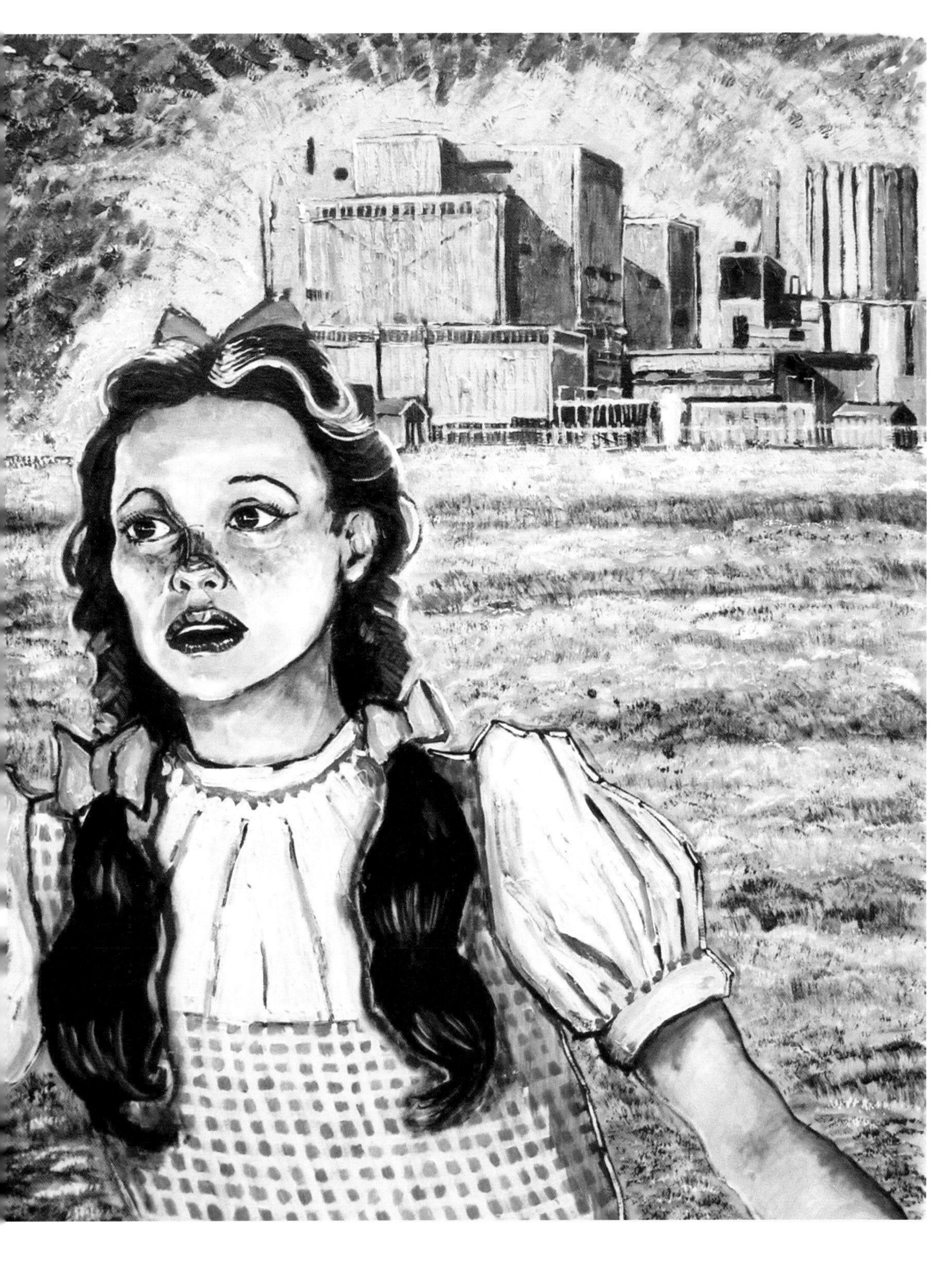

THE DUNGENESS LIGHTHOUSES

Dungeness lies at the southernmost point of Kent; it is an enormous flat triangle of sand and shingle, possibly the largest area of its type in the world. Because of its flatness and, until recently, lack of habitation, coupled with its many sandbanks, unpredictable currents and sudden changes in weather, the whole area has seen thousands of shipwrecks over the years with countless lives lost. The presence of a light at the end of the peninsula has been an important navigational aid.

Before any official lighthouse was built it is highly likely that the locals were paid to maintain a light (large bonfire) in order to warn shipping of the position of this highly dangerous hazard. As was the norm in those days, when times were hard (which they very often were), locals either 'forgot' to burn the warning fire or lit it somewhere else, giving a false impression of where the danger actually was. This practice became known as wrecking, for obvious reasons. The locals were then faced with a dilemma. They could either rescue the crew and passengers, hoping for a reward, together with any pickings that might be washed ashore, or – more often than not – they could murder any survivors and take everything.

An official Dungeness lighthouse was first mentioned around 1600 when Trinity House initially opposed a proposal for a light at Dungeness Point. Trinity House was a guild, or union, for pilots (it was thought that lighthouses would render pilots less important). However, Trinity House withdrew its opposition and an open coal fire was lit in 1615; the owner was allowed to charge one penny for every ship passing the light.

It was very difficult to collect the toll and, after an attempt to catch up with non-paying ship owners in port, these ship owners rallied together to have the lighthouse shut down as a nuisance, because of its poor and erratic light. As delivering coal to such an out of the way spot was difficult, candles had replaced the original coal fire. Parliament became involved in the wrangle, and the owner of the light was warned that it had to be improved.

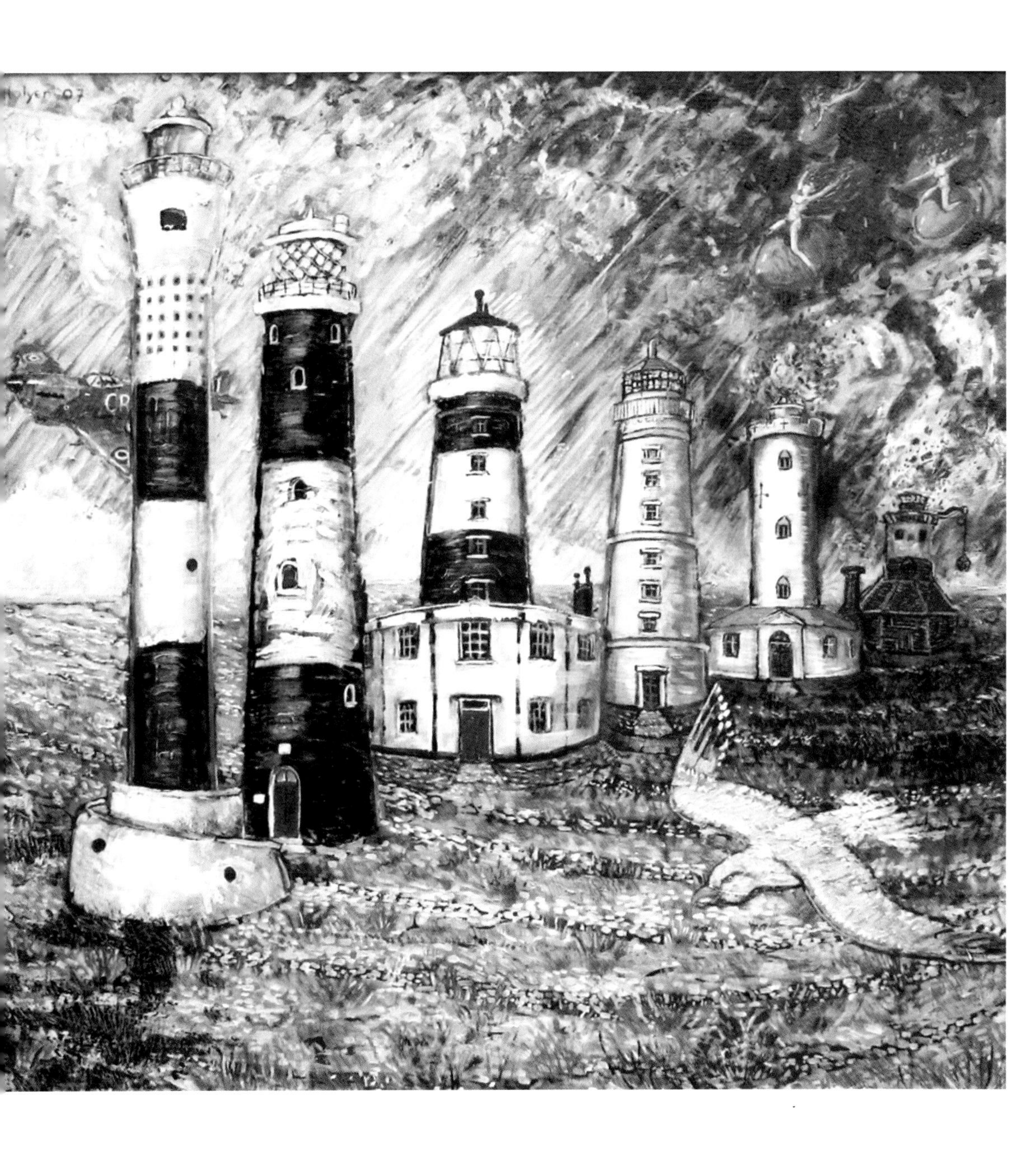
CR

Lamplough's Tower, 1635
Time had taken its toll, and as the sea receded further seamen complained of the distance of the lighthouse from the water's edge. In 1635 the patentee pulled down the existing tower and built a more substantial tower with a coal fire nearer to the Point.

The quality of the light once again came under review, and in 1668 Trinity House summoned the patentee to appear before it, insisting that he must provide better illumination.

A coal fire continued to light Dungeness in 1746, but the position of the lighthouse was complained of as being misleading as the sea had again receded, leaving the tower far from the water's edge.

Samuel Wyatt's Tower, 1792
In 1792 Samuel Wyatt built a tower about 115 feet high, of the same design as Smeaton's lighthouse on Eddystone, which lasted for over 100 years. Eighteen sperm-oil lamps took the place of the coal fire.

In 1862 Dungeness Lighthouse became one of the first lighthouses to be illuminated by electric light. However this form of power was superseded by a more efficient means, given the technology available at that time: a huge oil lamp of 850 candlepower surrounded by glass prisms that increased the illuminating power by a hundredfold. At this time the outer wall of the tower was painted black with a white band to render it more conspicuous in daylight.

Quarters for the lighthouse keepers were built in a circular form around the base of Wyatt's tower. Although the tower was taken down in 1904 these quarters are still in existence.

The High Light Tower, 1904
By the turn of the nineteenth century it was apparent that, once again thanks to the recession of the sea, a new lighthouse was needed. This circular brick structure, known as the High Light Tower, some 135 feet high and 36 feet in diameter at ground level, was completed early in 1904, and was first lit on 31 March in that year. Although no longer owned by Trinity House, this tower still remains at Dungeness.

The 1904 lighthouse now stands more than a third of a mile from the high water mark. Its navigational light was obscured by the nuclear power station erected approximately a quarter of a mile to the west of the lighthouse. This necessitated the placing of another light in a cylindrical tower just under 500 yards to the east, incorporating an electric fog signal.

The Present Lighthouse, 1961
The new lighthouse was officially opened by HRH The Duke of Gloucester and was brought into operation on 20 November 1961. The tower, which rises from a white concrete base in the form of a spiral ramp, is capable of automatic operation and was the first one of its kind to incorporate a Xenon electric arc lamp as a source of illumination. It is constructed of precast concrete rings 5 feet high, 6 inches thick and 12 feet in diameter, fitted one above the other, and has black and white bands which are impregnated into the concrete.

An additional point of interest is that since May 1962 the whole tower has been floodlit to assist identification from the sea. This floodlighting has reduced the bird mortality rate here during the migration season.

Dungeness Lighthouse was converted to automatic operation in 1991, and is monitored and controlled from the Trinity House Depot at Harwich.

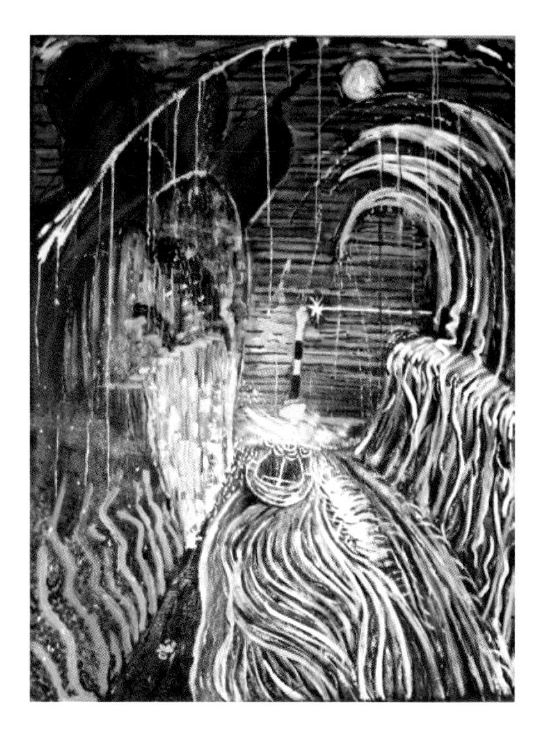

NORTHFLEET: NOTORIOUS HIT AND RUN

One of the most dramatic and hauntingly sad shipwrecks off Dungeness was the *Northfleet*. The *Northfleet* was a wooden three-masted sailing ship of 951 tons, laden with 340 tons of iron rails and 240 tons of other equipment to build a railway line in Tasmania, Australia. She was also carrying 379 people, most of whom were labourers and their families who were going to build the railway.

At about 10.30 pm on the night of 22 January 1873 she was at anchor just off Dungeness, directly opposite the Pilot Inn. (It is interesting to note that the *Northfleet* left Gravesend on 13 January; it had already taken nine days to travel some 60 miles by sea, on a journey that would take less than an hour by car today.) Her lights were burning brightly and it was a clear night with good visibility. A 300 ton Spanish steamer, the *Murillo,* basically cut the *Northfleet* in half and made off into the night, without stopping or making any attempt to raise the alarm or to save any of the 379 souls on board.

The heavily laden *Northfleet* sank within minutes, long before the other vessels at anchor around her realised that anything was amiss. There was considerable panic and Captain Knowles fought, revolver in hand, to keep back the crowd and save the women and children. Meanwhile the tug *City of London,* the lugger *Mary,* the *Princess* and a pilot cutter took off a number of people. There were many ships in the vicinity, but with the exception of these vessels they rendered no aid. The clipper *Corona* was lying at anchor only 300 yards away, but was unaware of the tragedy as the night watchman was asleep. Two other circumstances delayed rescue. Firstly Captain Knowles did not realise the extent of the damage and did not send up distress signals until fifteen minutes after the collision. Secondly the signal gun could not be fired owing to the touch hole being blocked. A survivor noted 'there was a terrible panic . . . among the strong, rough men, when it became apparent that the vessel was sinking. The wild rush for the boats, and the mad confusion which took place, were like the trampling of a herd of buffaloes.' Another survivor described meeting clusters of women as the ship went down, but 'did not stop to speak to them for I was looking towards the boats, thinking that I might get hold of one of them yet'. When asked by a mother to save her baby, he records, 'I could not do anything. For I felt the last had come.'

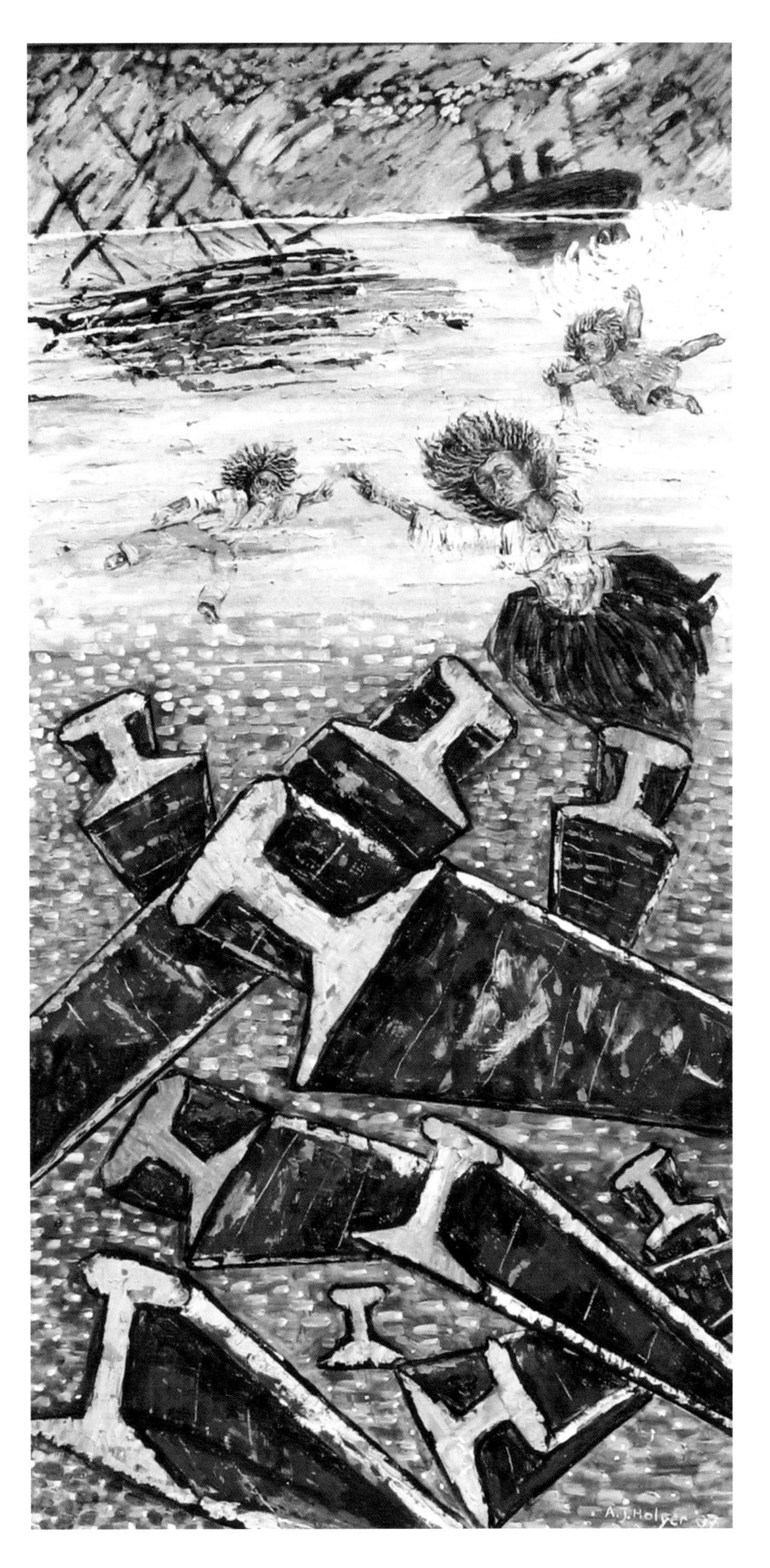
A.J.Holyer

When the cold hard light of dawn finally came, all that could be seen of the *Northfleet* was three huge masts sticking out of the water about a mile offshore, with a few wretched survivors clinging to them. Out of the 379 passengers and crew, 320 were drowned including Captain Knowles. Despite the gallant effort of Knowles and his crew, of the forty-two women and fifty-two children on board only two were saved. The terrible tragedy helped to arouse public attention, and led to the standardisation and enforcement of distress signals along with much more rigorous safety legislation.

The *Murillo* was eventually apprehended in Dover eight months later. A Court of Admiralty condemned her to be sold and severely censured her officers, including her commanding officer Captain Berrute.

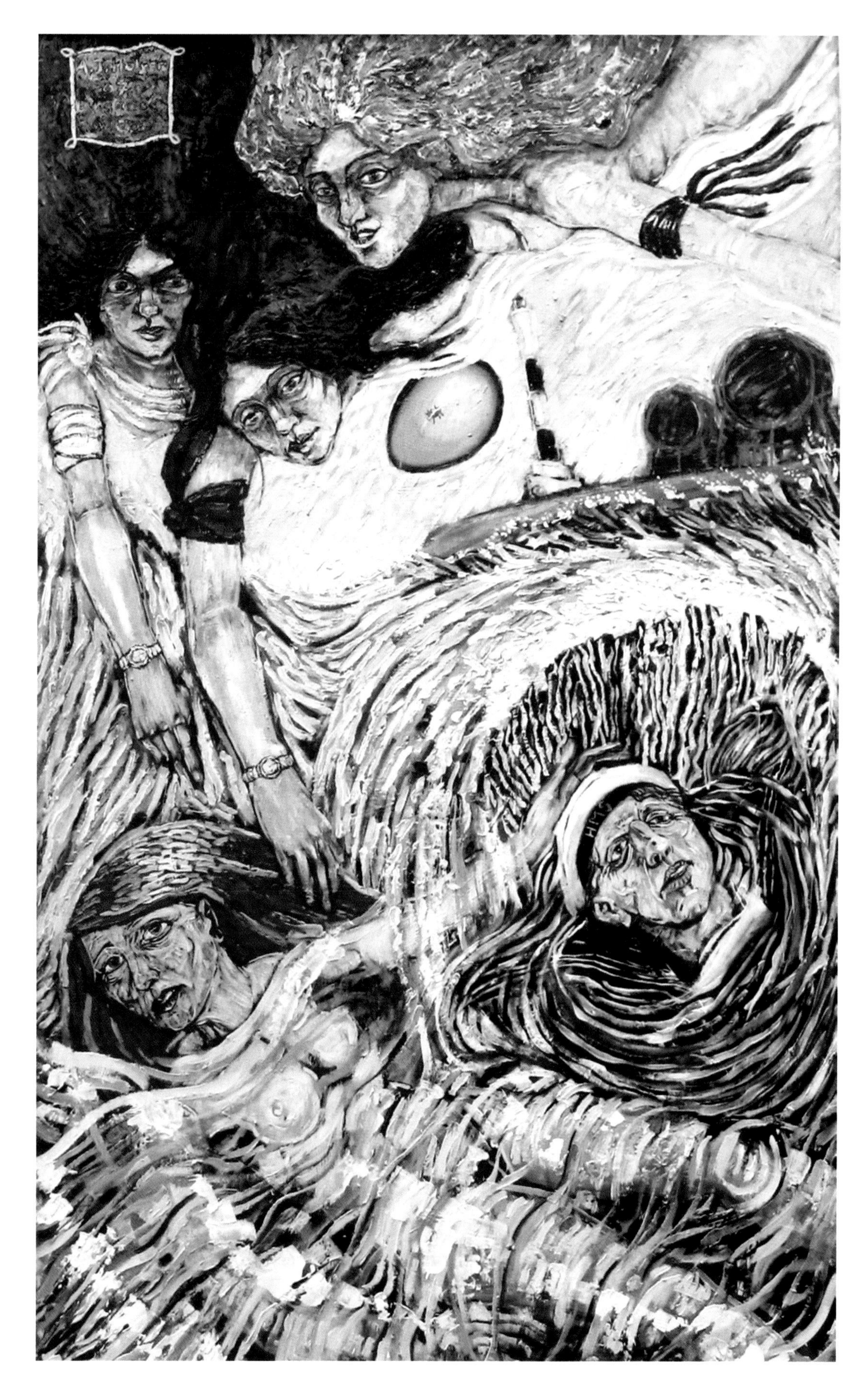

PLUTO

Today Dungeness looks peaceful, tranquil and unspoilt; this unique habitat is venerated and protected. Little more than sixty years ago it was not only one of the most heavily fortified coastlines on earth, but its landscape was also turned into a huge military engineering project that crisscrossed the area with pumps, pipelines and strange structures. The legacy of these endeavours is that even now some of the groundwater is contaminated with fuel. Sections of pipeline, some with oil or petrol still in them, are frequently pulled out of the shingle.

Pluto was until recently described as the outermost planet in our solar system, while some of you may be more familiar with the playful Disney dog known to millions worldwide. It is also the unlikely acronym for one of the most secret, technically brilliant and audacious schemes planned and actually completed during the Second World War. Without Pluto in place it is unlikely that the D-Day invasions would have been possible.

Pluto stands for 'Pipe Line Under The Ocean'. The war department spent many months trying to work out a way of getting the vast quantity of fuel and lubricants required to supply the invasion force to the French side of the English Channel. After months of rumination there was no clear solution until the chance involvement of Clifford Hartley, an engineer of over twenty-five years' experience in pumping fuel across some of the most hostile terrains on earth – although not under the sea. Hartley entered a room where one of the many fruitless discussions were taking place, and on seeing a huge map of the Channel on the table he asked what it was for. He was told that 'Mountbatten wants a pipe across the Channel, it's devilish urgent!' Within a few minutes Hartley had conceived and communicated the solution, to the amazement of the participants of the meeting.

Hartley's solution was to use the existing technology of underwater cable laying, which even back then had linked Britain and the US with many communications cables across 3000 miles of Atlantic ocean. He planned to use a modified cable, which was hugely reinforced on the outside but had no inner cable – thereby leaving a void through which fuel could be pumped at very high pressures to give the huge volumes that were required. These 'Hais' pipelines were laid using a conventional cable-laying ship. Much later in the proceedings engineers suggested using steel pipe unrolled from a large drum,

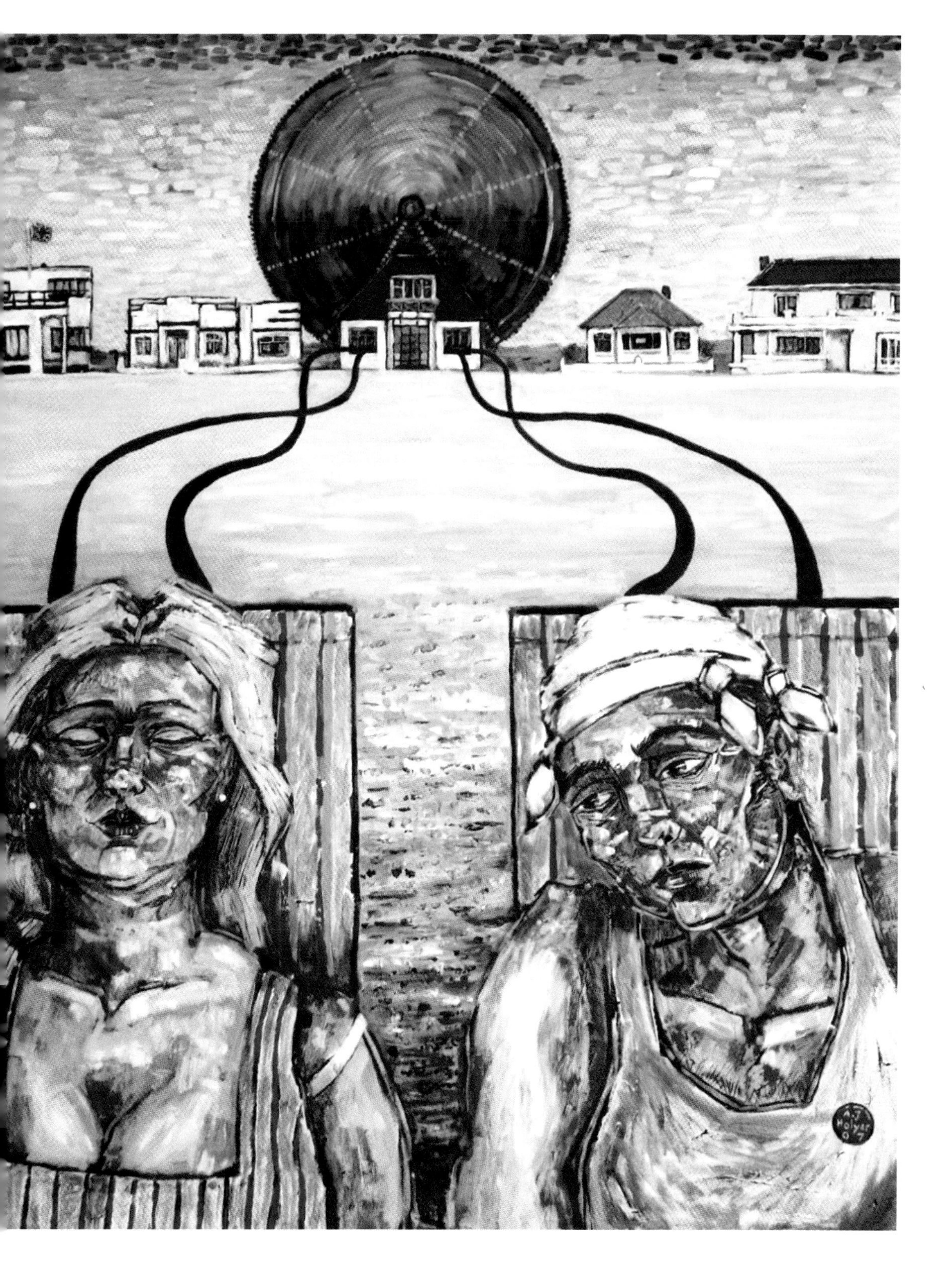
A.J.
Holyer
07

which would be much easier to manufacture. Trials were conducted and large floating 'Conundrums' were built to lay the pipe. This system was known as 'Hamel'.

The scheme required multiple pipelines, minimising interruption if one of the lines was discovered or damaged. A total of eleven Hais and six Hamel lines were laid. After D-Day the pipelines were regularly delivering over a million gallons of fuel a day across the channel. Amazingly they were laid under total secrecy right up to the French coast and under the noses of the occupying Germans. The Dungeness infrastructure of pumping stations and central control station was either hidden underground or disguised as bungalows and other domestic buildings. The Pilot Inn had a PLUTO pumping station hidden in one of its outhouses.

Today the pumping stations and other buildings have been converted into domestic residences which are difficult to identify from the outside. But most residents of a PLUTO property will tell you that they are easy to identify from the inside. The walls are usually over 3 feet thick and made of reinforced concrete, making some of the rooms much smaller than they appear from the outside. They are very difficult to heat during the winter as the walls are so thick, but they remain pleasantly cool in the summer. It is virtually impossible to put a picture or curtain rail up as the concrete is so hard. There is a section of PLUTO pipeline on display in the garden of The Pilot, and many other sections support the network of small bridges across the dykes and ditches of the Marsh.

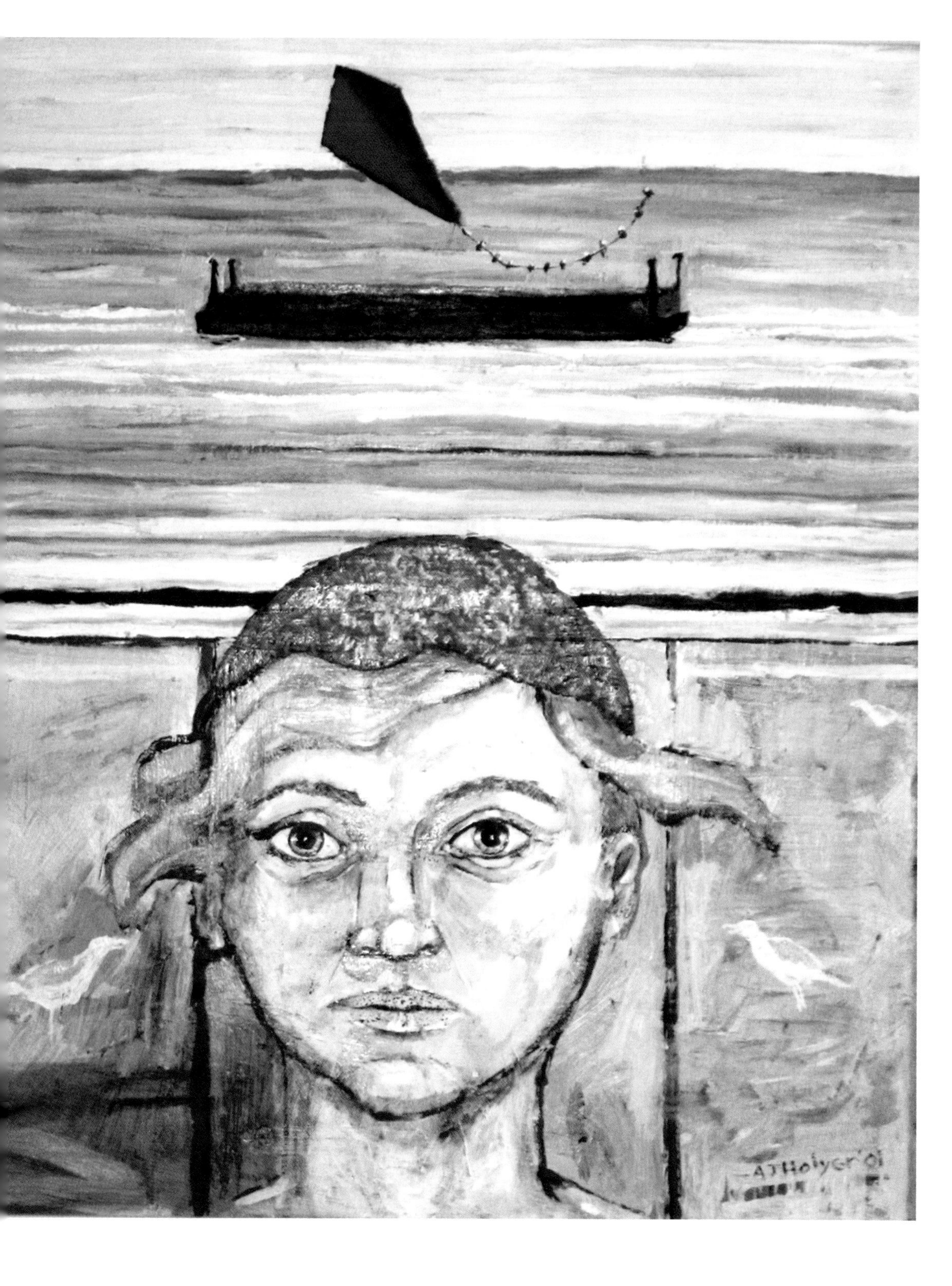
AJHolyer'01

PAYING ATTENTION TO THE LISTENING EARS

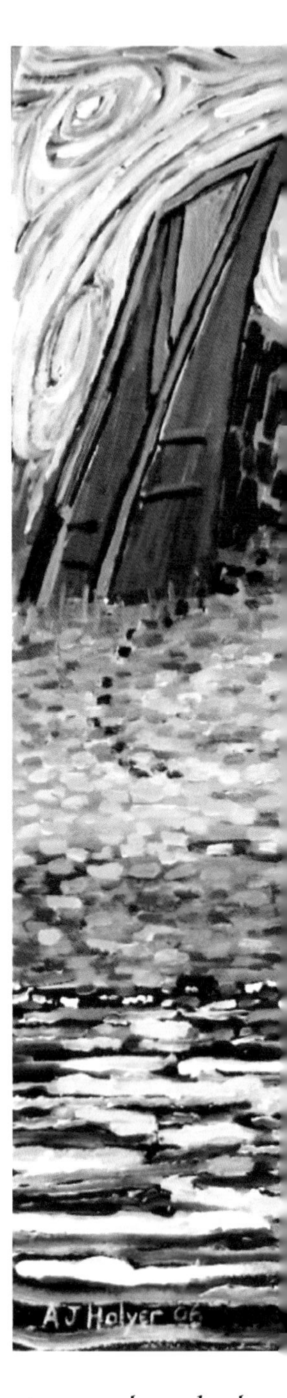

The listening ears were built during the 1920s. They are situated about half a mile inland at Greatstone. This lonely site, in the middle of the great expanse of shingle on Dungeness, is the only place in the world where all three types of listening ear can be found in the same place.

The term listening ears is a local one, and in many ways characterises the timeless, lonely solitude of these structures. The proper name for these sentinels of past ingenuity is acoustic sound mirrors.

The system was experimental, and presumably because of secrecy and to minimise noise pollution it was built in remote coastal locations, well away from prying eyes and industrial noise. These very sensitive listening devices were passive, which means that they did not send out any signals but attempted to listen for incoming aircraft, using a variety of reflector shapes to funnel the sound waves to a microphone. The output of the microphone was connected to a set of headphones and some electronic wizardry, which enabled the operator to plot a rough direction and sometimes even distance of incoming aircraft.

The job of the operator would have been cold, very uncomfortable and lonely, having to spend many hours in total silence entombed in concrete or in a remote wooden shed. One of the downfalls of the system was that it was very prone to sound pollution. A popular local story recounts how an operator was nearly deafened (some say he nearly died of a heart attack) when the local milkman rode his horse and cart along the coast road in line with one of the mirrors.

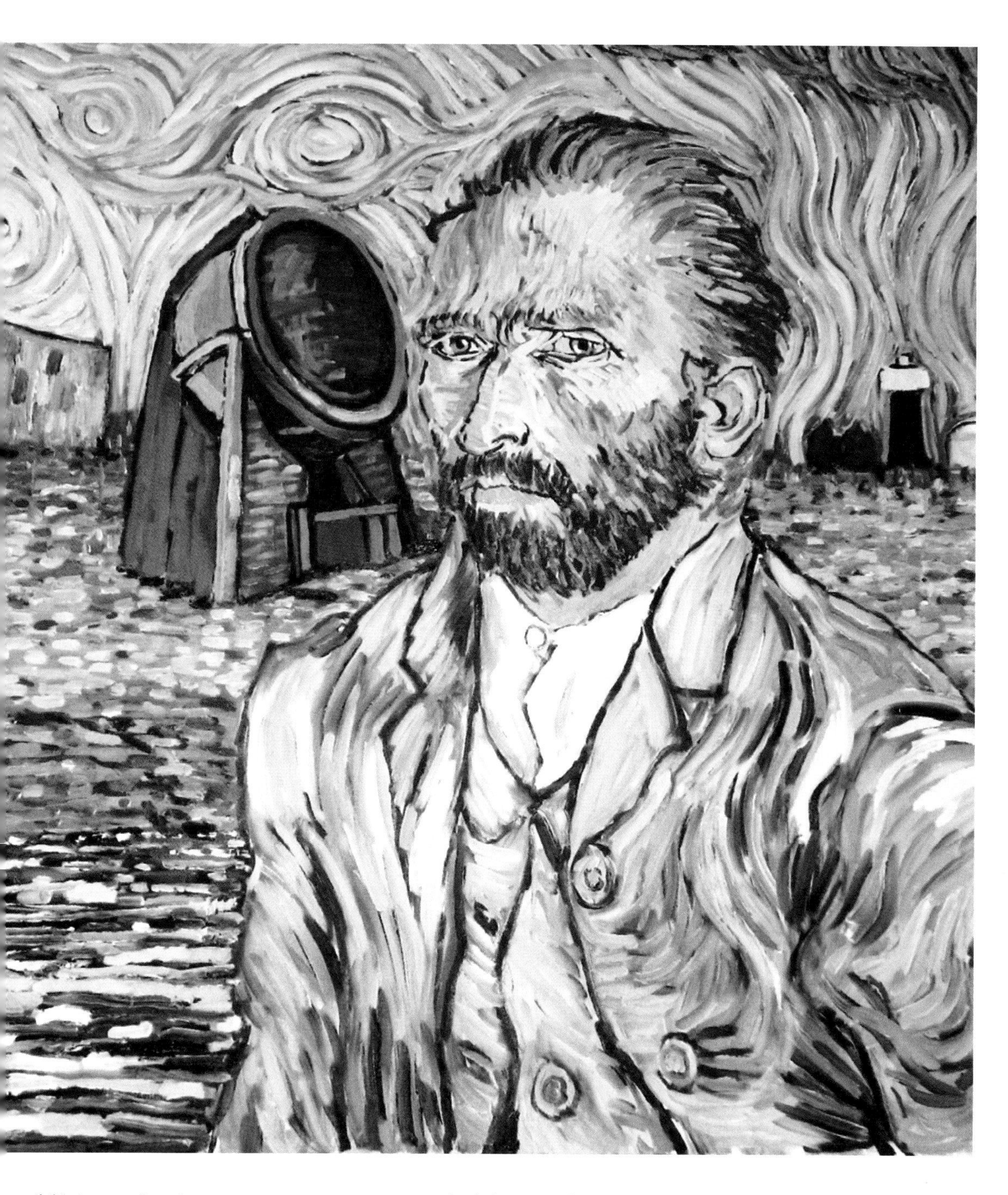

Ultimately the system was superseded by, and helped to inspire, radar. The system of disseminating intelligence through telephone substations and command posts was established by the sound mirrors team, and is now familiar to us from Second World War films in which WAAFs are portrayed monitoring aircraft movments on a large tabletop map.

THE LITTLE TRAIN

The Romney, Hythe and Dymchurch Railway, or RHDR as it is also known, has an interesting and distinguished history.

The railway was the realisation of a dream of two very rich eccentrics, one Captain J.E.P. Howey and Count Louis Zborowski. Zborowski was a famous racing driver who owned and raced the Mercedes called Chitty Chitty Bang Bang.

The name Chitty Chitty Bang Bang has origins which do not sit comfortably with its status as a children's favourite. The expression was coined during the First World War, when troops who had survived months in the appalling conditions of the front line were occasionally given the rare chance of a few days' leave. Their favourite destination was the bright lights of Paris. The leave document that they were given was known as a chitty; I will leave the Bang Bang bit to your imagination!

Unfortunately Zborowski was killed at the Monza Grand Prix before the first two locomotives were finished and before a site for their railway dream had been secured.

Undeterred, Howey enlisted the help of the designer of the first locomotives, one Henry Greenly (the leading designer of his day), to find a suitable site. Romney Marsh was quickly identified and a line was built between Hythe and New Romney. This opened in 1927, with an extension to Dungeness opening two years later in 1929.

Initially the 13½ mile railway was very successful, helping to fuel the dream of developing the south-east coast of Kent into a classy holiday resort. Unfortunately the advent of the Second World War put a stop to those dreams.

Amazingly the train was requisitioned by the war department and was instrumental in building the PLUTO pipeline. A special branch was laid to the site of the listening ears. Troops were billeted at the holiday camps and special trains were run for them. One of the locomotives, *Hercules*, was heavily armoured and equipped with two armoured bogie wagons that were fitted with anti-aircraft guns; they were even credited with shooting down an enemy plane.

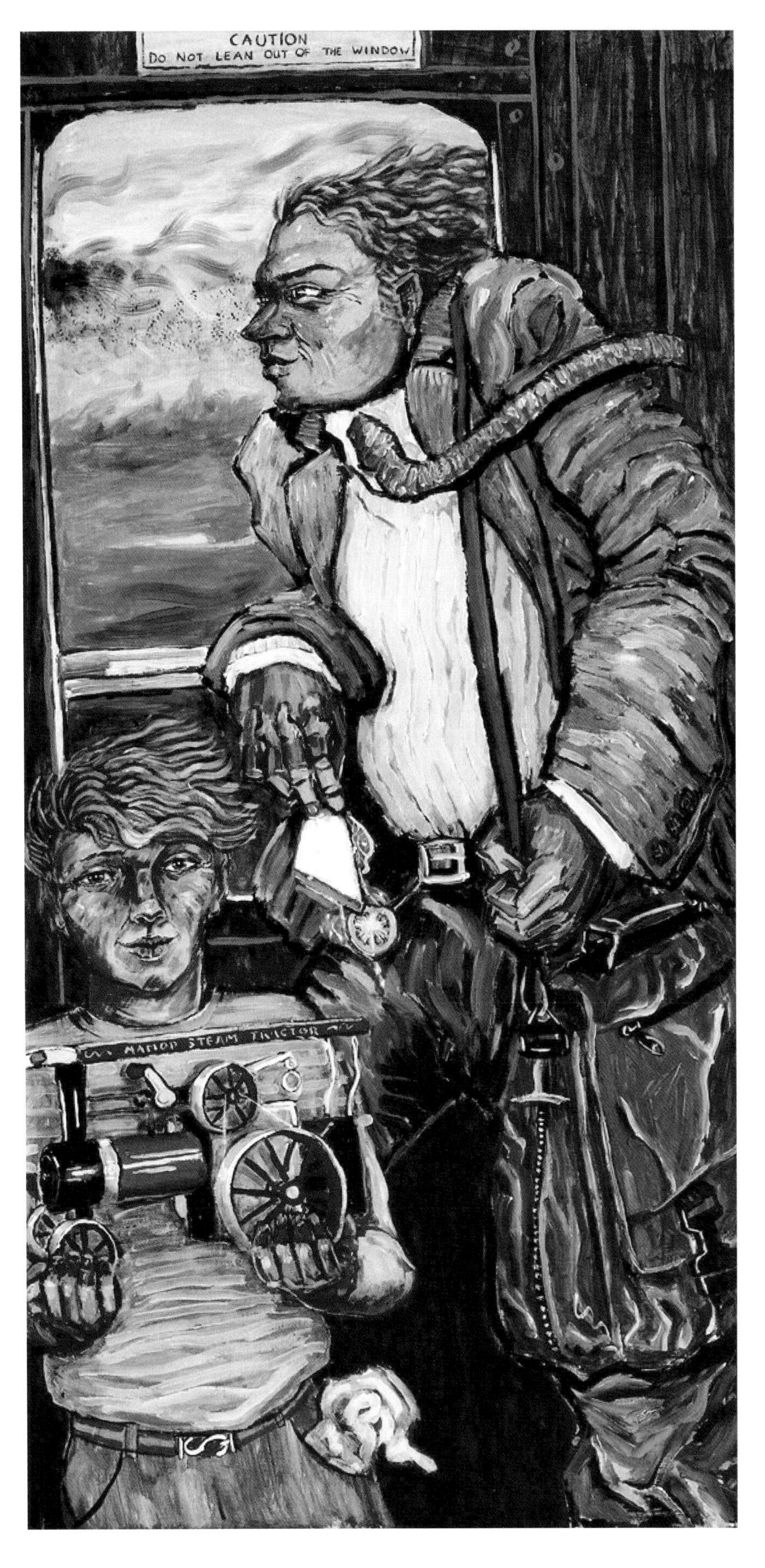
CAUTION
Do NOT LEAN OUT OF THE WINDOW
STEAM TRACTOR

Ultimately, however, the PLUTO project cost the railway dearly. The project involved miles of pipeline being welded together on the platforms at New Romney, and coaches were stripped down to the chassis to carry them. After most of the coaches had been destroyed it was found to be easier to drag the pipes across the shingle behind tracked vehicles; these destroyed the tracks and footings as they went.

After the war the RHDR was handed back to the owners in a very sorry state. Undeterred, they rebuilt the line and rolling stock, and the last section of track to Dungeness was officially reopened by Laurel and Hardy in 1947.

Interestingly, the Pilot Inn was at one time the only pub in Britain with its own railway station (the Pilot Halt). Unfortunately the station was closed in the early '80s because of road safety concerns.

Although initially the railway was very successful, the advent of cheap package holidays and the death of Captain Howey in 1963 saw a huge decline in passengers, and the RHDR deteriorated to the point that it was effectively bankrupt. The railway was saved in 1973 when Sir William McAlpine stepped in; it has not looked back since.

HOLY STONES AND HAGSTONES

Hagstones, which are also known as Holy Stones, Holey Stones, Epilates Stones, Wish Stones, Nightmare Stones and Witch Riding Stones, are stones that have a hole running all the way through them. They are found in some numbers on the Dungeness shore, if you know where and how to look. The Dungeness stones are exclusively of flint which has been washed out of the chalk cliffs along the whole of the south coast of England.

There is some speculation as to how the holes are formed. Most locals believe that the action of the sea causes a small stone to eventually wear a hole through a larger stone. One of the local names for hagstones is 'pregnant pebbles', as there are often baby pebbles trapped in the hole of the larger stone. My own take on the formation of some of the hagstones, which is based on observations and discussions with geologists, is as follows. Many stones seem to have some organic contamination included in them at their formation, millions of years ago; for instance a piece of wood or even a dead sea creature. As the stone wears naturally through sea erosion, the contaminant is exposed and is a weak point in the stone. This area is composed of softer material, so the sea is able to quickly erode the weaker part, thus leaving a hole. I have found many stones that exhibit signs of fossilised shells and anemones which are partially or totally holed.

Locally it is customary to thread holy stones on a cord; some consider that fourteen stones threaded together are very lucky.

It is a common belief that magic cannot work on running water. Because these stones have been holed in running water they are supposed to retain that influence, and therefore protect from magic.

Through many of the world's cultures and back into prehistory these stones have been used ritually to protect people and animals from the powers of evil spirits and witches, and were often worn around the neck, or hung on the key or door to the cattle stalls or stables. Hagstones were also thought to prevent milk from curdling during a thunderstorm, when evil spirits were most active. This practice continues today in parts of Britain and Europe. In some parts of Europe farmers milked their cows so that the milk passed through a hagstone.

Many disorders were thought to be cured by hagstones. Placing them under the bed was thought to relieve cramp and rheumatism, while they could prevent internal disorders that were caused by hags sitting on the stomach during the night.

In *Brand's Antiquities* we find the following quote: 'A stone with a hole in it hung at the bed's head will prevent the nightmare. It is therefore called a Hag Stone from that disorder which is occasioned by a Hag or Witch sitting on the stomach of the party afflicted. It also prevents witches riding horses, for which purpose it is often tied to a stable key.'

In parts of Scandinavia a large quantity of ale poured through a hagstone was given to an expectant mother to ease birth pains. An Arabic custom was to tie a hagstone around the neck of young camels to protect them from evil spirits and the evil eye. In some parts of Britain hagstones were fastened to the bows of boats to keep them safe when at sea.

An interesting custom was the use of hagstones as pledge stones, which were held to ensure a person was telling the truth. Perhaps the most interesting properties a hagstone was thought to possess were the ability to enable the bearer to see the faerie folk, and to be protected from their enchantments. For a hagstone to keep its full power it was supposed to be found by the bearer or given in love.

Larger hagstones were used for weather magic. A cord was threaded through the hole and tied, and the stone was then swirled vigorously around the head at arm's length in order to dispel winds and rain clouds.

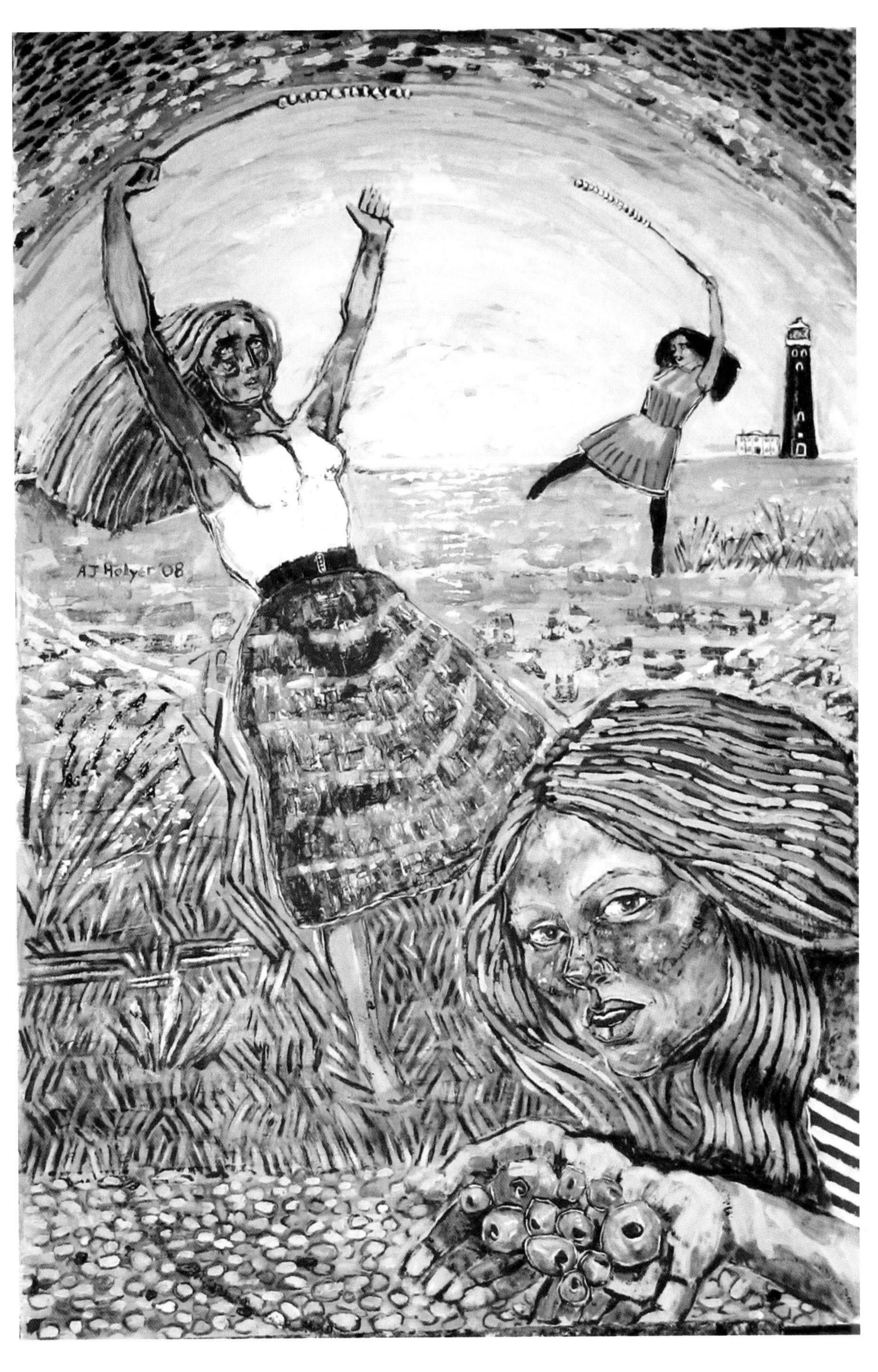
AJ Holyer '08

SAINTS CRISPIN AND CRISPINIAN

Dungeness lies at the extreme south-east corner of the British Isles; it has always been a place of mystery and intrigue. Geographers and geologists say that until recently (600 years ago or so) Dungeness was an island or a narrow spit of shingle over 4 miles long jutting out into the English Channel. Drainage or 'inning' joined it to the mainland proper in the last 500 years. Yet going back well over a thousand years there have been stories of some kind of stone monument on the end of this shingle spit.

There are many old legends which state that St Crispin and his brother St Crispinian were martyred after a series of grisly attempts at their execution, sometime in the third century AD. First they were stretched and bound to a tree, and were beaten with staves, then awls (which shoes were sewn with) were threaded and put under the nails of their fingers, and sewn to strips of skin which were cut out of their backs. But as the brothers prayed during their ordeal the awls sprang from their nails and struck the torturers, wounding them cruelly. Then Rictius Varius (the Roman governor) commanded millstones be hung round their necks, and that they be drowned under the winter ice of the river Axion. However, the water did not drown them, and they cast off the stones and walked to the other side of the river, bathing as if it was midsummer. When Rictius Varius saw this miracle he was enraged, and commanded that a vat of lead be melted in a fire and the holy martyrs be cast into it, therein to be drowned and consumed. But the holy men, praying and chanting whilst being immersed in the molten lead, caused a drop of the hot metal to spring into the eye of Rictius Varius, blinding him. He obviously did not get the message as he then commanded pitch, oil and grease to be boiled; the holy men were thrown into the mixture to be drowned and consumed. But the saints continued to pray as they bathed in this acrid, caustic bath, and as soon as their prayer was finished an angel led them out of the vat without injury. When Rictius saw this he threw himself in the fire, and there perished 'by the righteous judgement of God'. Once Rictius was gone the holy men prayed that they would be delivered of their torments and meet their maker. This duly occurred when Maximianus (the emperor), hearing of the death of Rictius, had their heads cut off and their bodies cast into the sea. They floated away and landed on Dungeness, where a stone monument was built to inter their remains.

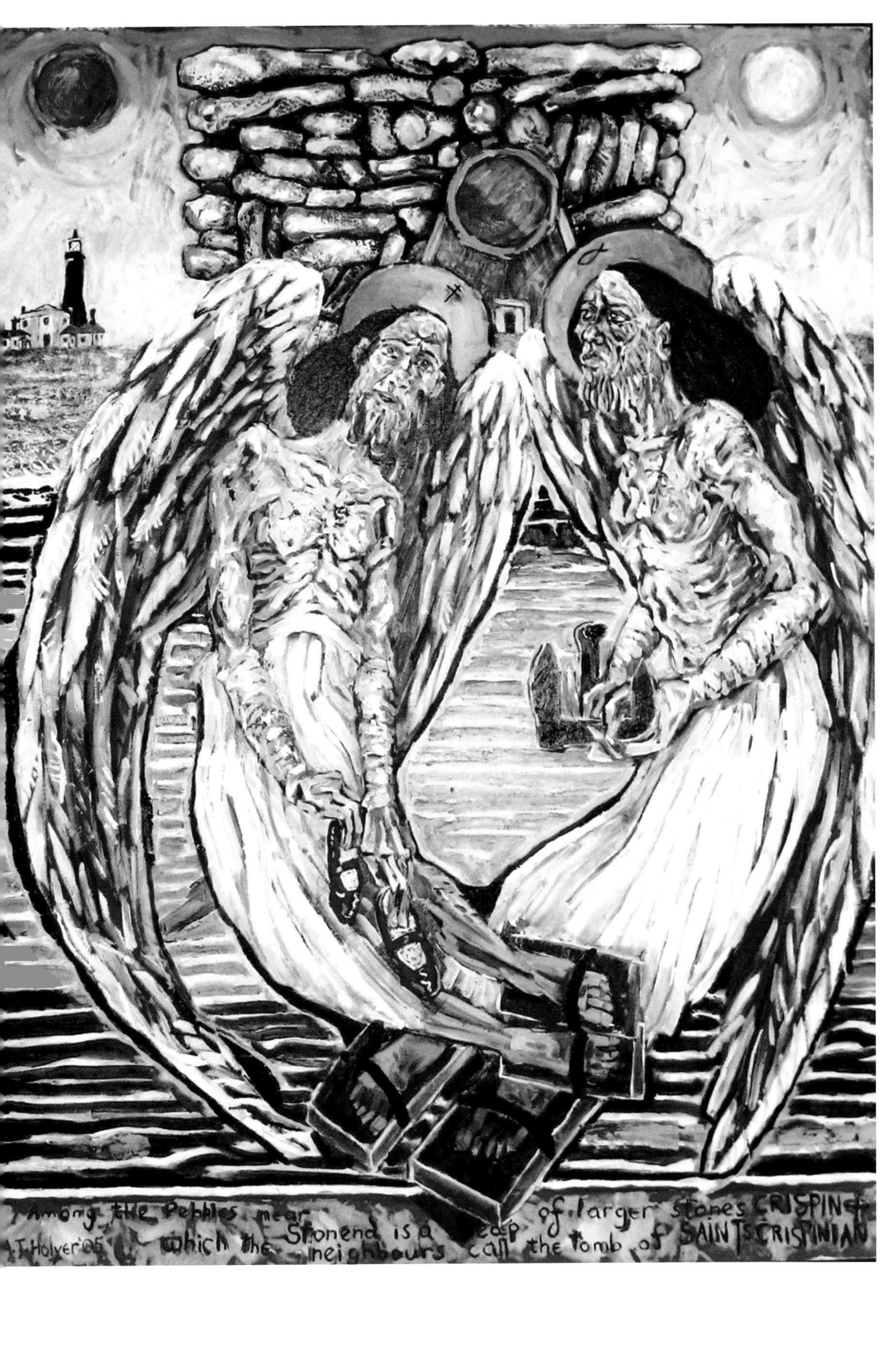
Among the Pebbles near Stonend is a heap of larger stones which the neighbours call the tomb of SAINTS CRISPIN & CRISPINIAN
A.T. Holyer '05

Their story, as with many other saints, is possibly one of pre-Christian gods, kings and monuments, woven into Christian mythology. As there are no reliable records it is difficult to unravel fact from fiction, but we do know that there was a large heap of stones or stone monument on the seashore directly south of Lydd. This monument was locally known as 'stone end', was traditionally the tomb of Crispin and Crispinian and is recorded on Speed's map of 1612. It no longer exists and it is difficult to place its exact location, although it is mentioned as still being extant in the late eighteenth century. It is possible that the stone was used to build some of the Napoleonic fortifications, possibly on the same site.

Why was the monument built in such an inaccessible and remote location? One of our theories is that on the midsummer solstice the extreme northerly travel of the sun just touches the point of Dover when viewed from this location. It then travels back south across the sea for the rest of the year.

THE ANASTASIA ENIGMA

One of the strangest and as yet unresolved enigmas connected with the Fifth Continent concerns the Grand Duchess Anastasia , and the speculation that not only did she survive the murder of the Romanovs, the Russian royal family, but that she lived out her last years in Lydd, and is buried in the town's cemetery. Far fetched? read on.

On 17 July 1918 seven Romanovs and their household staff were bundled into their basement and shot dead by Russian revolutionaries.

Over the years there was speculation that at least one of the family escaped, and various unsubstantiated claims were made on the Romanov legacy. There was no real evidence to support this, or any reason to believe that anyone had escaped the execution. That is until 1991, when the bodies were finally exhumed and DNA tested using a sample from HRH Prince Philip (the Tsarina's great-nephew). Five bodies were confirmed as Romanovs, but the bodies of the Tsaravich and one of his sisters werer not found with the other victims in the mass grave.

Although there have been many claimants to the Romanov dynasty over the years, one of the few remaining possible candidates is Larissa Feodorovna, who is buried in Lydd cemetery.

Neither Larissa nor her husband Owen Tudor made any claim that she was the Grand Duchess Tatiana, nor is there any hard evidence that she was, but her story is very strange and does leave many unanswered questions.

The information available from the time indicates that Owen met Larissa in 1921 in Constantinople, where he was posted with the army; apparently she was working as a belly dancer. When he finished his posting he brought her back to England with him. She seems to have been spirited into the country, as there is no sign of her on the immigration files.

This is incredible in itself, as the extremely tight immigration restrictions of the day meant that it was virtually impossible for anyone to enter the country without first being intimately scrutinised for suitability, former occupation and poor health. Larissa had TB, which would have barred her entry to England. Furthermore, even if she had been spirited in the wagging tongues of the day would soon have exposed her and had her thrown out.

Not only did she arrive and stay, Larissa also married Owen Tudor in 1923, when he was twenty-two. It was prohibited for an army officer to marry until he reached the age of twenty-eight, and even then the potential wife had to meet certain criteria. Being a former belly dancer would have made the marriage impossible. The marriage certificate states that Owen Tudor was 'of independent means', yet it is known that he had no other income other than his Army salary.

When Owen married his former belly dancer he was not thrown out of the army but posted to the sleepy town of Lydd, until the death of Larissa in 1926 – when he was invited to rejoin his former regiment. In the stiff, formal atmosphere of the '20s this sequence of events should have been virtually impossible, and one would have expected it to cause uproar at every stage.

Larissa's headstone in Lydd may give some clue to her true identity. It does not take the surname of her husband, nor does it bear her maiden name Haouk; instead it has the name Feodorovna, which is a name uniquely used by the female side of the Romanov royal family.

The grave itself is an enigma. Over the years it has been tended and renovated by unknown persons.

Could Lydd be the last resting place of Princess Tatiana, the last Romanov?

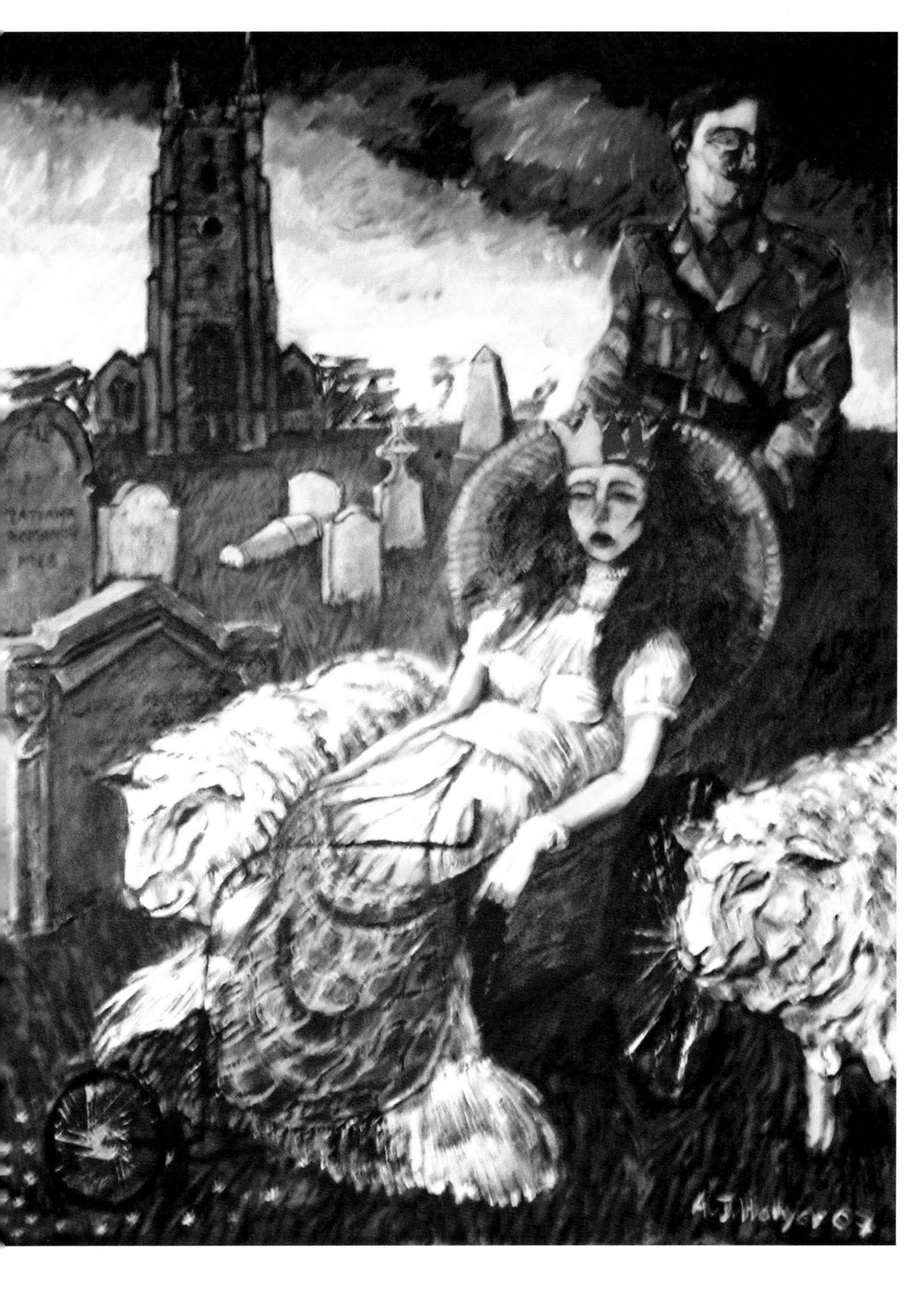
A.J. Hollyer 07

THE SHIP INN, DYMCHURCH

Dymchurch is a small holiday resort, and 'children's paradise' which owes much of its fame to the Doctor Syn novels written by Russell Thorndyke, erstwhile actor and imaginer of the Marsh's murky past. The Ship Inn was his favourite pub and by observing the regulars he formed the characters that would populate his many books.

The Ship Inn itself, dating back to the 16th century, has a legitimate history of smuggling. Indeed more recent restoration has revealed secret chambers and indications of concealed tunnels. It stands opposite New Hall, a court of the Brotherhood and Guestling of the Cinque Ports, who administered the autonomous power of the Marsh. The church of St Peter and St Paul is also nearby. It is here that the shadowy cleric Doctor Syn, a.k.a. 'Pirate Clegg', had his power base.

Whilst the 'good' vicar Syn is a fictional character, Dymchurch can boast of a real heroic priest. In 1867 a great storm burst on the channel. In its thrall a French lugger was wrecked on Dymchurch Sands. Lives were at risk and the coastguard, John Batist, tried in vain to swim out to the men with a lifeline. On seeing this the Dymchurch vicar, Charles Cobb, plunged into the roaring waves to assist. After many attempts, the vicar and coastguard managed to drag the one remaining survivor to safety. Both received medals.

No account of Dymchurch, the Marsh or Doctor Syn is complete without a resounding rendition of Captain Clegg's 'quaint old capstan song':

Here's to the feet wot have walked the plank -
Yo-ho! for the dead man's throttle.
And here's to the corpses afloat in the tank,
And the dead man's teeth in the bottle.

For a pound of gunshot tied to his feet,
And a ragged bit of sail for a winding-sheet,
Then the signal goes with a bang and a flash
And overboard you go with a horrible splash.

And all that isn't swallowed by the sharks outside,
Stands up again upon its feet upon the running tide;
And it keeps a-blowin' gently, and a-looking' with surprise
At each little crab a-scrambling' from the sockets of its eyes.

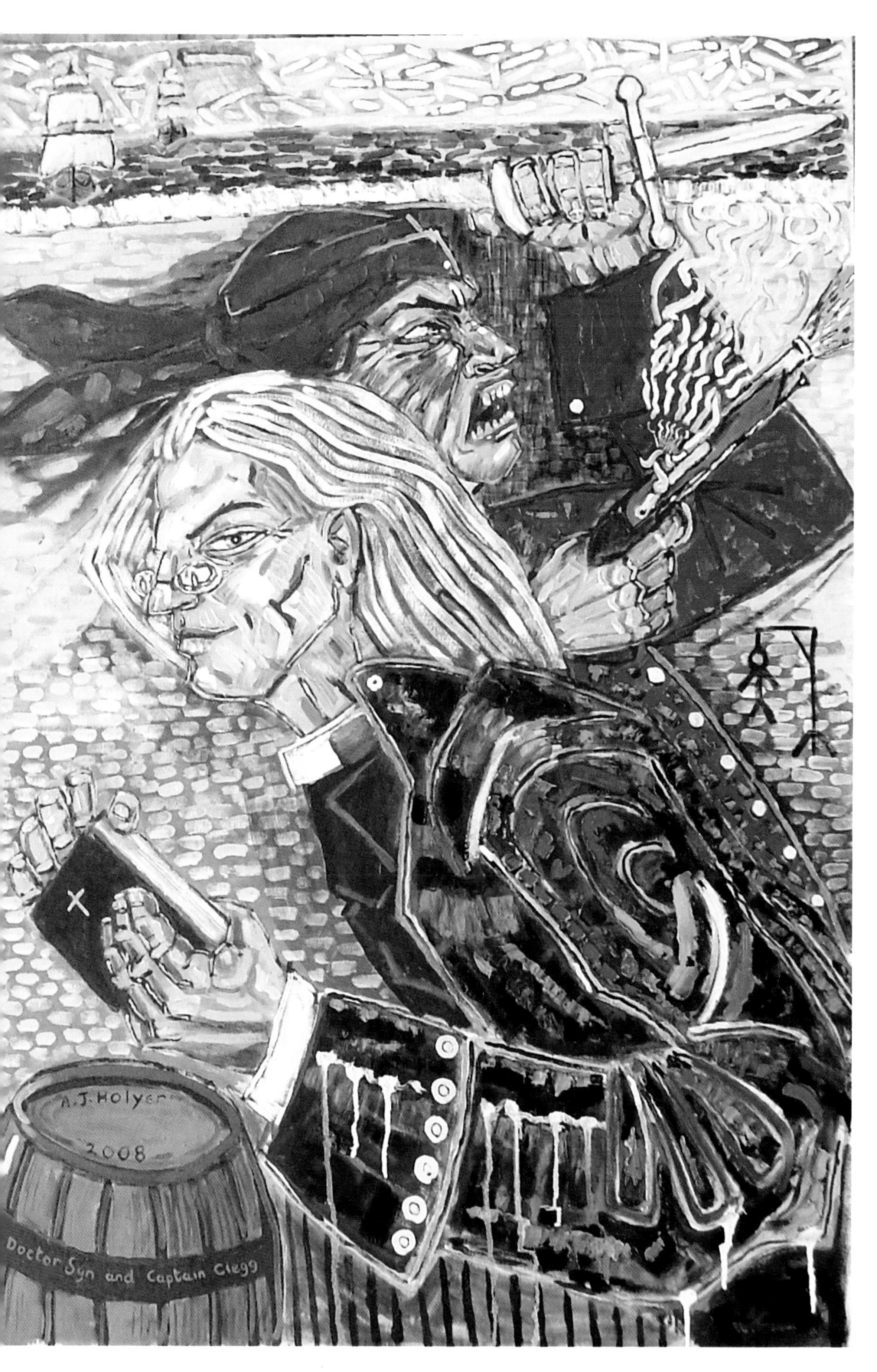
A.J.Holyer
2008
Doctor Syn and Captain Clegg

POETS AND PAINTERS

Dungeness [John Taylor, A Discovery by Sea 1580 - 1653]

Like rowling Hills, the Billowes beate and roare
Against the melancholy Beachie shore,
That if we landed, neither strength nor wit
Could save our Boate from being sunke or split.
To keepe the Sea, sterne puffing *Eols* breath
Did threaten still to blow us all to death,
The waves amaine (unbid) oft boorded us,
Whilst we almost three hours beleaguered thus,
On every side with danger or distresse,
Ressolv'd to run on shore at *Dengie Nesse.*
There stand some thirteen Cottages together,
To shelter Fishermen from winde and weather
And there some people were as I supposed,
Although the dores and windows all were kept clos'd:
I neere the land, into the Sea soone leapt
To see what people those same houses kept,
I knock'd and cal'd, at each, from house to house,
But found no forme of mankind, Man or Mouse.

This is the earliest piece of writing that I know of depicting Dungeness. It is remarkable that little has changed in four hundred years! We still find residents of Dungeness fugitive. I lived there for a few years but knew fewer people. The attraction and point of Dungeness is its isolation which residents guard diligently.

Today there is a small population of artists, writers and intellectuals living in the now highly priced 'cottages' at least for weekend sojourns from London displacing the original fishing community who have dispersed to more comfortable accommodation along the coast. It is however a population not a community. There is no artistic school of Romney Marsh or Dungeness, nor has there ever been.

But many creative spirits have found inspiration here, and expressed the strangeness and compelling allure of the Marsh. Amongst those who have created literature and art amongst the pebbles and dykes of the marsh are

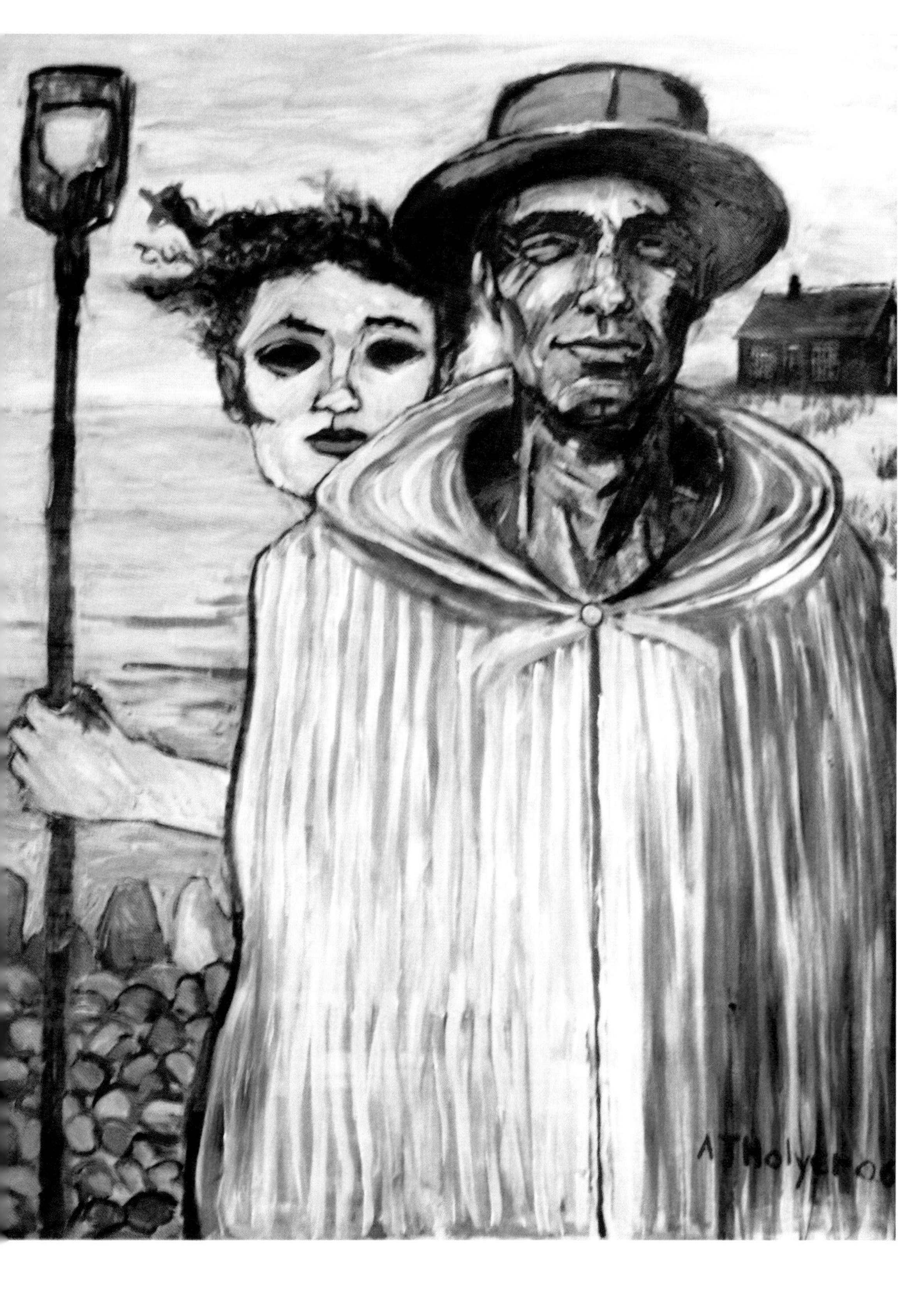

Henry James, E F Benson, Joseph Conrad, Radclyffe Hall, Stephen Crane, Edith Nesbitt and latterly the filmmaker and gardener Derek Jarman.

Paul Nash and John Piper are forbears of the contemporary painterly population who forage the beach for driftwood and dreams. Looking to the big skies and long vistas they all found a canvas in which to express their particular sensibilities.

John Piper compared Dungeness to an "oversized nursery floor littered with coastguard cottages, huts, stores, lighthouses and flagpoles." Whilst Noel Coward [who wrote his early plays in St Mary in the Marsh] described the sky over the marsh [doubtless cigarette holder in hand and smoking jacket bound] as "Too red. Very affected."

Reginald Turner in 'Vision of England' was appalled and shocked to his tweed socks to observe that "There are also holiday camps, sites for caravans and all the trappings of gregarious amusements which are so unfortunately enemies of beauty. One has to admit that Romney Marsh is horribly blemished by shacks and shanties."

I prefer the writings of those who accepted the Marsh for what it was and is and speak affectionately of it. Probably the most famous literary and cinematic celebration of the Marsh are the smuggling novels written by Russell Thorndyke in The Ship Inn at Dymchurch concerning the adventures of Doctor Syn. These stories are now so well known that most tourists believe Doctor Syn to be a true historical figure. They can be forgiven for thinking so as within the Marsh tales of smuggling are as common as hawthorn, sheep and the flight of the heron.

A 'real' local smuggling family were the Sisleys of Lydd whose descendants include the French impressionist painter, Alfred Sisley.

The essential plot of Doctor Syn novels is of a pirate who reinvents himself as a vicar, leading a band of smugglers dressed at night as phantoms who weave in and out of the mists and winding lanes of the Marsh. "Sufficient for us that the marsh is ruled by a power - a mysterious power - wot brings gold and to spare to the marsh man's pockets...no one knows better than you do that she's a queer sort of a corner, is Romney Marsh. I've seen you a-prowlin' and a-nosin' about her...The marsh don't approve of folk a-nosin' and a-prowlin'

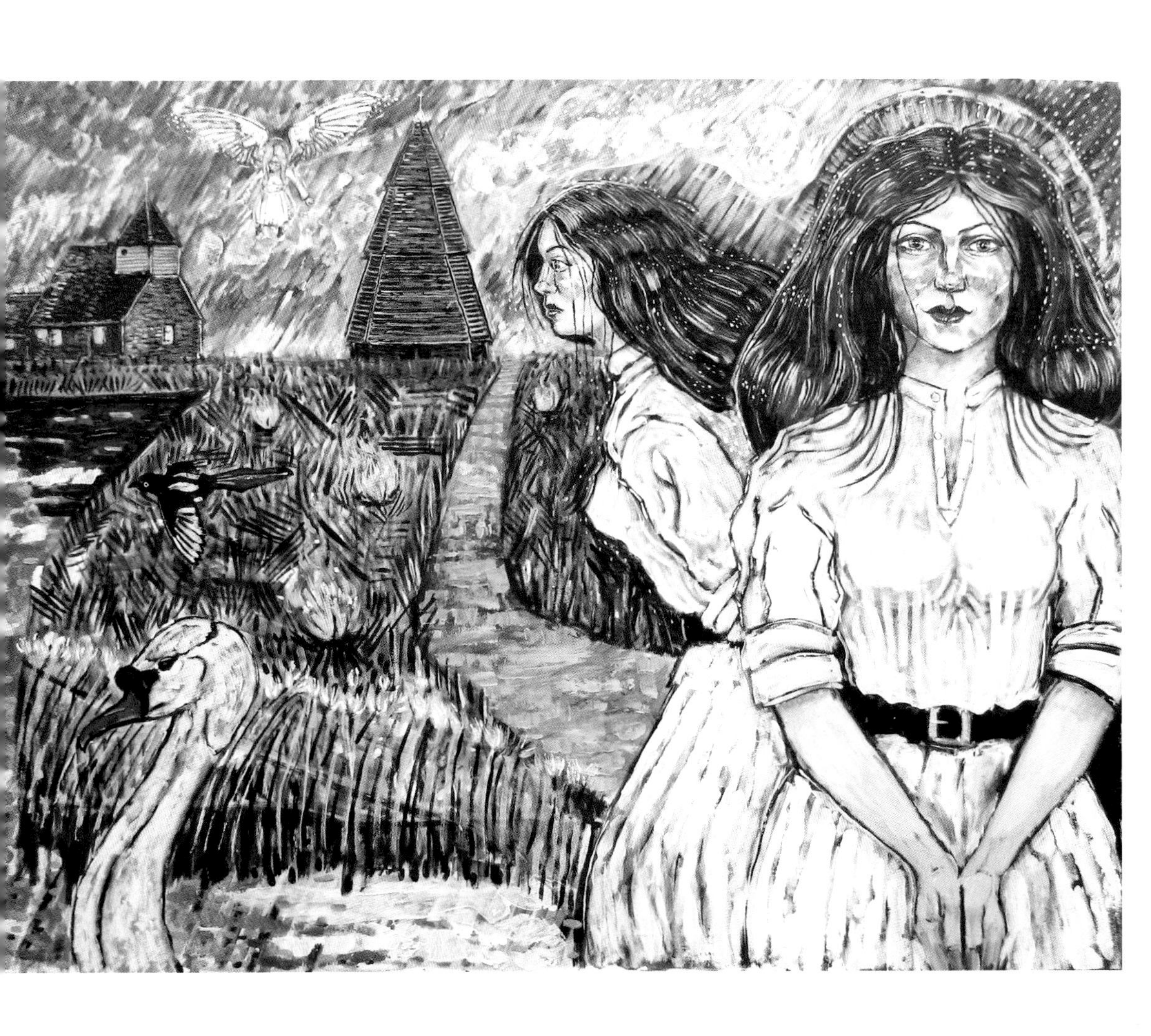

after her secrets, see?" And the sextons face grew suddenly fierce. All the lines of quizzical humour vanished from around that peculiar mouth and left a face of diabolical cruelty, cunning and malice'.

There is a hint of Treasure Island 'Boys Own', swashbuckling bravado about these stories and little wonder that filmmakers like Disney and Hammer put the characters into the cinema.

A more authentic novel set upon the Marsh and also made into a movie [screenplay H E Bates, score by Vaughan Williams, starring Googie Withers 1948] is 'Joanna Godden' by Sheila Kaye Smith. It was first published in 1921, but set prior to the Great War. It s tempting to describe it as an early feminist novel as its main protagonist is a farmer who battles against the prejudices of the local male farming establishment.

"Joanna Godden was big - not just fat, but broad and large boned as well. She was also what was used to be known as 'common', even vulgar, showy, blowsy...The power and strength of the woman, her 'wholesome splendour', persists like a glow in a fire, damped down for the night, but ready to roar again the next morning."

"Now the folks around here there middling sensible" she says "but they aint what you call clever. Theyre stuck in their ways, you might say." Dangerous talk.

One of the delights of the book, as well as descriptions of familiar locations on the Marsh is the author's attempt to write dialogue in the vernacular.

"Joanna Goddens a woman, fur all her mans ways, and you cant expéct her to have präaper know wud sheep."

In the novel, Joanna is cast out of Marsh society, gaining an illegitimate child but losing her farm. The 1948 movie however celebrates her as a strong woman who effects changes on agriculture and society. In a post war world of black and white austerity and social reform and when land girls and Rosie the riveter where recent memories, this is a fascinating piece of propaganda.

From the same period, we have 'Kipps' by H G Wells. Kipps can also be read as either socialist propaganda or as a good yarn, which has also had its cinematic interpretations. The story of an aspiring draper's assistant set

largely upon the Marsh and Folkestone, it contains many passages of description of Dymchurch, Littlestone and Dungeness.
For me it is notable for my family's one and only mention in English literature when, as a child, Kipps fights the local butcher boy who is carrying "Mrs Holyer's leg of mutton."

No account of literary associations with Romney Marsh would be complete without mention of Rudyard Kipling. Whilst he lived just over the border in Sussex, he drew much inspiration from the Marsh. In 'Puck of Pooks Hill' he adopts Barham's "fifth quarter" into the "sixth continent" and goes on to describe the Marsh thus. "The Marsh is just riddled with diks an' sluices, an tidegates, an water-lets. You can hear 'em bubblin' and grummelin' when the tide works in 'em, an' then you hear the sea rangin' left an' right-handed all up along the wall. You've seen how falt she is - the Marsh? You'd think nothen' easier than to walk end-on across her? Ah, but the diks an' the water-lets, they twist the roads about as rarelly as witch yarn on the spindles so 'ye get all turned round in broad day-light."

I know the feeling.

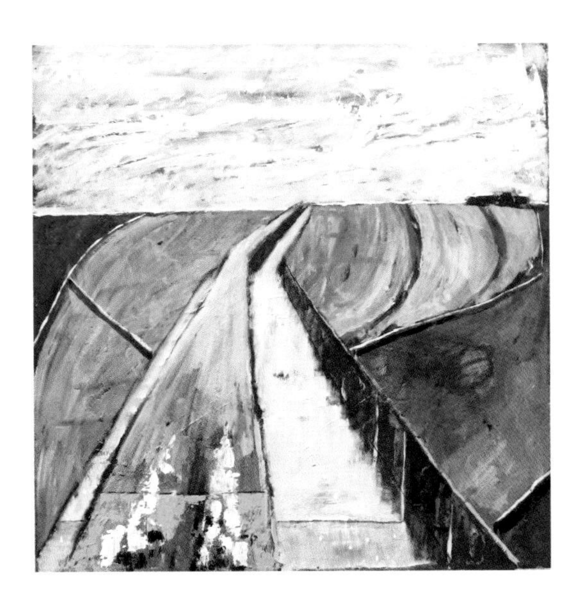

His poem 'Brookland Road' in which he sees the ghost of a lost love [arguably a metaphor for the loss of his son in the great war] inspired one of my paintings. His most famous poem pertaining to the Marsh and all things smuggled has to be 'A Smugglers Song' with this well known refrain.

Five and twenty ponies
Trotting through the dark -
Brandy for the parson
'Baccy for the clerk;
Laces for a lady; letters for a spy,
And watch the wall my darling, while the gentlemen go by!

Those of us addicted to the Marsh will sympathise with Ford Maddox Hueffer writing in exile from the eminently lumpy and bovine Switzerland.

God, to be in Romney Marsh
And see the ships above the wall -
I'd give these lakes and Alps and all
For just an hour of storm and shower,
And just a glimpse of Lydd church tower,
And just to hear the wind in the thornes -
Just not to hear the cowbell's din,
Just not to hear the cowmen's horns -
But just to mark the tide come in,
Dear God by Dymchurch wall.

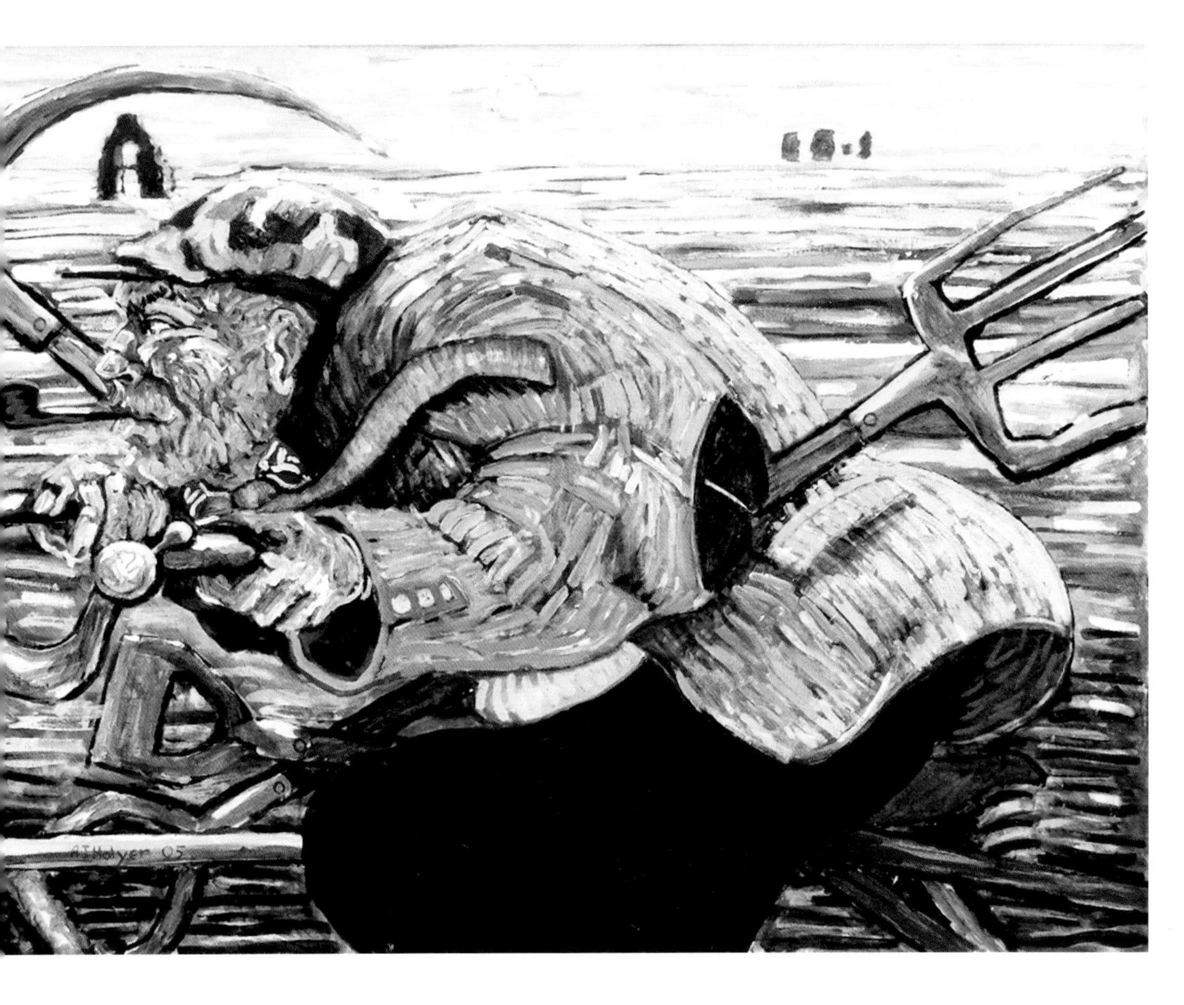

OLD ROMNEY

Although loosely based upon an old photograph of my Grandfather, this painting is inspired by another.

I have never met the gentleman but most residents of the marsh will recognise this image of a man steadfastly cycling across the marsh in all weathers. Always with pipe in mouth, weighed down by the tools of his trade, he travels from smallholding to smallholding.

He epitomises, in some way, the spirit of the marsh, the locus genii, the embodiment of our ancestors and we hope our descendants.

Andy Holyer, August 2008

LIST OF ILLUSTRATIONS

BIBLIOGRAPHY

Suggested further reading

Camden, Thos *Britannnica* Hutchinson 1997
Carpenter, Edward *Romney Marsh in Old Photographs* Sutton Publishing, 1994.
Carpenter, Edward *Romney Marsh, a Second Selection* Sutton Publishing, 1996.
Carpenter, Edward *Wrecks and Rescues off the Romney Marsh Coast* Margaret Bird, 1985.
Eddison, Jill *Romney Marsh, Survival on a Frontier* Tempus Books, 2000.
Finlayson, Iain *The Sixth Continent* Atheneum, *1986.*
Hillier, Caroline *The Bulwark Shore Eyre Methuen, 1980*
Ingoldsby, Thomas *The Ingoldsby Legends* Circa 1840.
Ingram, Richard & Piper, John *Pipers Places* Chatto & Windus, 1983.
Jarman, Derek *Derek Jarman's Garden* Thames & Hudson, 1995.
Jerrold, Walter & Thomson, Hugh *Highways and Byways in Kent* Macmillan & Co, 1907.
Kaye-Smith, Sheila *Joanna Godden* Cedric Chivers Ltd 1921.
King, Greg, and Wilson, Penny, The Fate of the Romanovs, John Wiley and Sons, Inc., ISBN: 0-471-20768-3 (Romanov)
Kipling, Rudyard *Puck of Pooks Hill.* Macmillan & Co, 1906.
Main S. P. B. *The Land of the Cinque Ports* Christopher Johnson, 1949.
Piper, John *Romney Marsh.* King Penguin, 1950.
Lockyer, Herbert *Psalms, A Devotional Commentary* Kregel Publications 1993
Randle, Dave *Romney Marsh Past and Present.* Sutton Publishing, 2005.
Read, Herbert *Paul Nash* Penguin Books, 1944.
Thorndike, Russell *Doctor Syn* Rich & Cowan, 1915.
Turner, Reginald *Vision of England.* Paul Elek, *1950.*
Wells, H. G. *Kipps* Schreiber & Sons, 1905

Websites

www.lifeonmarsh.co.uk
www.thepilot.uk.com
www.andyholyer.com